UNITED STATES FOREIGN POLICY

ACROSS ASIA

Ramesh Raizada

Create Space
An Amazon Company

Dedication

I am dedicating my book to my parents-Shri Kishen Narain and Shrimati Chandervati. I am deeply indebted to my mother who gave me hope, courage and inspiration.

Acknowledgements

Special thanks go to my daughter Nishi and my son Avinash for their enthusiasm and encouragement. I want to express my thanks to my wife Rekha for her continued support. Many thanks to Satish Narayan, Andrew Mutch and Editorial staff of Create Space for their friendly and valuable suggestions.

CONTENTS

PREFACE

PREFACE

Our ever changing world presents unique challenges every day; it never ends. No atomic bombs are falling but iconic changes are taking place around the world whether we are noticing them or not. Asia has taken the center stage of the global political arena. Just a decade ago, historians would not predict that China would become the most nerve wrecking adversary economically and militarily against the United States in Pacific Asia and else where. The foreign policy planners sitting in Washington D.C have to turn their pages from European Union and NATO to stormy and dangerous rising tides of South China Sea and chilly and deserted mountains of Afghanistan. During the last fifty years nothing dramatic has changed in the European landscape. Relations between the western countries and the United States have remained on the same level of trust and co-operation. The foreign policy pundits are chanting the same old mantras. But that is not true in case of Asian sub-continent; every country is requiring individual attention and special consideration.

President Obama and Secretary of State Clinton have repeatedly mentioned in their policy statements that United States has to shift its foreign policy emphasis from Europe and Middle East to Pacific and South Asia. Countries like China, India, South Korea and Indonesia are bound to take important positions in U.S foreign policy planning. Iraq and Afghanistan have taken an unnecessary toll on United States resources; they would be exited from major decision making process. President Bush made a major political blunder in invading Iraq and prolonging war in Afghanistan. The American vision of implanting democracies in these two countries would be difficult to achieve. Iran, on the other hand would continue to demand U.S and western countries vigilance. North Korea and Iran have become the major source of worry not only to the United States but to the whole world.

When we look at U.S foreign policy in Asia, we have to analyze the regional influence of China and Russia in the Far East and Central Asia. At the present time, Russia does not have any heavy weight affect on any Asian country. China on the other hand has started exerting its due influence in the region. Consider Afghanistan and Pakistan, in this context. It seems likely that Afghanistan would lean towards U.S.A but would not rule out China and Russia, at the same token. Pakistan is a solid supporter of China block and it would like to get support from the United States, as well. In this scenario, the United States has to be very careful when dealing with Pakistan. China needs a densely populated and highly militarized country like Pakistan as leverage against India. Pakistan serves China's interest very well and it needs China help in a possible dispute with India. Under these conditions, United States has to review its foreign policy from time to time. Pakistan has been playing a double role for many years. At the same time, it has become very important in terms of solving Afghanistan problems. It is very likely that after United States leaves Afghanistan in 2014, Taliban would take over the country with the help of the Pakistan army. It would be sad ending for the United States as well as for the rest of the world. Afghan people would face the dire consequences of this tragedy.

The objective of the foreign policy of the United States is to turn as many countries favorable to its point of view as much as it is possible and feasible. Sometime, it becomes very difficult to achieve that goal. Disagreement between staunch allies is very much a reality. The recent economic and financial crisis in the world markets is a true indicator of how the world leaders perceive a brimming catastrophe and react to solve the situation differently in their own way. What is considered good for America may not be perceived good for other countries even though they may be friends of the United States. Many European do not want to see a shift in the American foreign policy towards Asian continent. But as realities stand today, there is absolutely no chance of going back for the United States, from the central stage of the Asian world. The future world will be dominated by the Asian countries and not by the European nations. This notion is embedded in the thinking of the American leadership and it is going to stay that way in the future planning process. China, India, Japan, Korea and Indonesia will play major role in the global say; there is no second opinion about it. If the United States could make more friends among non committed nations like Indonesia, India and Malaysia, it would be considered a winning trophy.

Russia may be receding from the Asian scene but China plus Russia may be emerging from the horizon. The economic clout of China and military might of Russia could dictate the terms of Asian stability and peace. China in its own standing can make a big difference in the future political structure of East and South Asian countries. In other words, United States should be ready to face the potential threats from China in the very near future.

It is very much a good possibility that China and India might challenge each other at some future dates in history; backing from the United States to India would be a critical consideration in such a scenario. India and China, down the road, would be invincible opponents and consequently they might bark a little bit but would not venture to bite.

History might not repeat itself all the time; Imperialist China may not like to follow the Japanese colonialism. But it would like to have a great say in the affairs of Asian countries like Burma, Cambodia and Laos. However, it might not interfere with Viet Nam, Thailand and Indonesia. In the event of any conflict between China and the United States, Viet Nam is likely to give its support to the United States and not to China. Taiwan is the sore point between China and the United States and most probably it would continue to have uncertain future. China would not start a war with the United States on Taiwan; at the same token, United States would not force Taiwan to provoke China. The status quo condition is likely to stay in position.

Thailand had been a steady ally of the United States. However, in the recent years, Thai government has shown some leaning towards China. Thailand is the only country in Asia which remained independent and never came under any European power. The foreign policy of the United States should put more emphasis on improving relations with the Thai government and down grade the Chinese influence on the country; that should be the U.S strategy.

Our study does not include Arab nations in the Middle East and Africa. President Bush wrote in his memoirs that history will judge his actions in Iraq; he wanted to see Iraq as a model democratic country for the rest of the Arab countries. An Iraqi citizen said" What democracy? U.S removed Saddam Husain but to see democracy in Iraq is a long distance dream". The Arab Spring Revolution starting from Tunisia to Egypt, Yemen and Libya and spreading to Syria had no connection with the U.S invasion of Iraq. So far monarchies in Saudi Arabia, Jordan and Morocco have escaped the wrath of bloody uprisings and consequent repression. These newly emerged so called free from dictatorship regimes have a long way to go before they would establish themselves as real democracies. These countries need lot of financial assistance and well laid out plans to move in the right direction. The future is unpredictable and there might be numerous problems on the way.

The world is no more a bi-polar world; the Russian influence in the Middle East and other Asian countries is almost negligible. There are no indications that any other country would fill in the shoes. China will rise gradually to the status of a Super power but will not be able to displace the United States for a long time to come; the chances are that it may never able to take the American place, militarily and financially. It does not mean that United States just sit on its laurels and do nothing worth its established traits and characteristics. The fifteen trillion economy has to move forward vigorously and leave others far behind. Only then, United States could keep its status as a sole Super power. Along with this resolution, the country has to plan a broad based mutually beneficial foreign policy towards other countries as to create more friends and allies not only in Asia but through out the world.

A pivotal foreign policy decision has to be made regarding Israel and Palestine. At least three U.S presidents had tried to bring peace to the thorny problem of Israel and Palestine but failed in their efforts. All the anger and violence from the Muslim world had its origin from the land of Palestine. United States has been blamed for following pro-Israel policies and at the same time, Iran vows to wipe out Israel from the face of the earth. Under these conditions, it is not an easy task to formulate a policy that might serve the purpose of the United States as well as Palestine. Either Iran has to change its policy or Israel might destroy all the nuclear installations of Iran. The prospects of a peaceful resolution of this problem are dim. The American foreign policy for this region would be tough to implement and might require lot of expertise.

If our world has to have peace and prosperity for most of its people, it has to find some common denominators that could make it happen. Multi-cultural values in life, religious tolerance and appreciation for others and liberal thinking would go a long way to bring the different communities of the world together. The foreign policy of the United States has to address this delicate and potentially dangerous situation before it is too late.

ALLIES
THAILAND

Siam now called Thailand means land of the free. It is the only country in Asia which was not subjugated to the European colonialism. It is a beautiful country with some of the most beautiful temples in the world. Buddhism came to Thailand more than two thousand years ago from India; 95% people are Buddhists.

Thailand neighboring countries are Burma in the north, Laos and Cambodia in the east and Malaysia and Singapore in the south. Till 1980, it was mainly an agricultural country but now it is a vibrant industrialized country. It is the largest exporter of rice in the world; Tin, Tungsten, rubber, top quality lumber and Tuna are other large export items. Electronic, textiles and auto parts are leading the export list now.

The present population of Thailand is sixty eight millions (2010). The Gross Domestic Product is 320 Billions. The Gross National Income per capita is $4.5k and the literacy figure is 95%. The rate of growth varied from 3.5 to 7.5%.

Thailand stands on three pillars; they are Monarchy, Military and Buddhism. Though it has Constitutional Monarchy, however, the king is a powerful political authority in the country. After the King, military junta plays a decisive role in the government affairs. Elected leaders have been displaced by the military coups many times; the latest event took place in 2006 when Prime-Minister Thaksin Shinawatra was removed by the military generals. Thailand and Turkey are in the same boat where military is the dictating force.

Bangkok, the capital of Thailand is very popular with the foreign tourists. It has the world's largest night club and many most luxurious hotels. There is a growing gap between the upper rich and the bottom poor .Considering other neighboring countries like Burma, Laos, Cambodia and Viet Nam, Thailand comparatively is well off. The unfortunate part is that it has become a prominent sex trade center. HIV diseases have spread and it has taken a heavy toll on human lives. Poverty in the rural areas is the major cause of this wide spread sex industry.

In 1997, like many other countries of South East Asia, financial crisis hit the economy of Thailand and general public wanted a change. The populist leader Thaksin Shinawatra won the election by a huge majority in 2001. However, a bloodless military coup in 2006 removed him from his job. A new constitution drafted by the military in 2007 helped the leader of the opposition party Vejjajiva Abhisit to become the new Prime-Minister. Fresh elections were held in 2008 and very interestingly the youngest sister of Thaksin, Yingluck Shinawatra won the elections solidly and became the first female Prime Minister of Thailand. She is only 44 years old and had never held any public office before. The country is badly divided between rich middle class and rural poor class. How the inexperienced Prime Minister bring together the two warring sections of the country will make a big difference in the prosperity of Thailand.

Relations with Asian Countries

Japan: Thailand and Japan have sustained long lasting monarchies. The relations between the royal families of these two countries are very cordial and friendly. The king and the queen of Japan attended the 60th Coronation ceremony of King Bhumibol of Thailand. These long lasting solid relations between the heads of these countries have paved the path of strong economic and commercial interactions. Japan is the number one investment source for Thailand and number two for imports and exports destination. There are no disputes of any kind-trade or territorial-between the two. With this background, it could be safely predicted that the future relations between the two countries would be smooth and progressive.

China: Thailand has a small-about 14%-Chinese minority. However, it has integrated into the main stream without any kind of discrimination. In fact, Sino-Siamese community is well placed in all walks of the nation-government, business and professional. Thaksin Shinawatra and AbhisitVejjajiva both belong to Sino-Siamese political families. Thaksin Shinawatra was promoting strong relations with Communist China. To please the Chinese government he had refused permission to Dalai Lama to come to Thailand and endorsed the claim of main land China over Taiwan.

It must not be forgotten that foreign policy of Thailand has always followed a policy of intelligent leverage. Thailand is a major Non NATO ally of the United States. In 2003, President Bush had visited Thailand and signed a strategic treaty for holding Cobra Gold Military Exercises which entitles Thailand to procure advanced military hardware. Thailand supported U.S.A in providing small contingent of military personnel in Iraq and Afghanistan. U.S.A is the second most important source for investment for the country. In other words, Thailand wants to be in good terms with China as well as the United States. Most of the Asian countries are weighing in the rise of the Chinese military and monetary power and are shaping their foreign policies accordingly. The future trajectory of Thailand foreign policy would be to balance the influence of China and the United States.

India: Hinduism and Buddhism migrated to Cambodia, Thailand and Burma from India centuries ago but in the recent times there are no big interactions between these countries. In 2007, Prime Minister of Thailand Ahisit Vejjajiva visited India and Dr.Man Mohan Singh, the Indian Prime Minister paid a visit to Thailand in 2006 to promote "Look East" policy. So far nothing spectacular has happened in terms of increased trade relations or any kind of strategic alliance between these two countries .It seems that Thailand is more interested in establishing strong relations with China and India is not going out aggressively to build a strong partnership with Thailand. The relations between the two countries are friendly and normal but there are no strong bonds and there are no disputes. If India wants to challenge the Chinese influence in Asia, it has to change its policy towards Thailand. India is in a good position to provide various kinds of assistance programs in Advanced Technical Education, Health

Care and Military Training. At the same token, Thailand has to give more attention in promoting Indo-Thai relations. It will be mutually beneficial

Philippines: After almost three hundred years of Spanish rule and fifty years under the United States, Philippine finally got its freedom after World War II. During its fifty years of reign in Philippines, United States did not improve its economical, medical and educational standards; no progress of special significance was made. However, English became the lingua franca of the country besides Spanish and Philippines became a special ally of the United States.

At the present moment, Thailand and Philippines have cordial and friendly relations. They celebrated 60th anniversary of establishing special fraternity ties between them. Japan's King Akihito visited Philippines and President Gloria Arroyo has visited Thailand to promote closer relations .There are no disputes between these two countries. Both countries are members of ASEAN community and are close allies of the United States.

Australia: Thailand has a good opportunity to work closely with the Australian government to improve its educational, medical and technical know how. The two countries have already signed a Free Trade Agreement treaty in 2005. The two way trade between the two countries in 2010 is hitting 20 Billion Australian dollars. About 400,000 Australian tourists visit Thailand yearly. The relations between the two countries are friendly and there are no disputes among them.

Thousand of students from India and China are enrolled in Australian Universities for higher education; Thailand should follow this path to develop a core group of highly educated elite. This is bound to help the Thailand economy in the long run. Currently there is an institute called Australia Thailand Institute that has been set up to upgrade the standard of higher education in Thailand. Australia does not have giant manufacturing organizations that could open facilities in Thailand. However, it is a rich country that could invest in Thailand's economy. The government should take steps to attract Australian investment; it would make a big difference in the national economy.

Indonesia: Thailand and Indonesia have some common political features. The military junta is very powerful in Thailand and till very recently, Indonesia was ruled by a military dictator General Suharto for more than thirty years. At present, Thailand has a democratically elected Prime Minister Yingluck Shinawatra and Indonesia too has a publicly elected President Yudhoyono. Yingluck is the first lady Prime-Minister of Thailand and happened to be the youngest sister of former Prime-Minister of Thailand Thaksin Shinawatra.

Thailand is facing some rebellion from the Muslim terrorists group in the region which is adjoining Malaysia. Yingluck realized the role that the largest Muslim country, Indonesia could play in controlling these militants group and she asked for his support. Thailand is also having problems with Cambodia on some temple dispute. President Yudhoyono, as the current President of ASEAN has assured the Thailand Prime-Minister to take steps to resolve this off and on border fighting between Thailand and Cambodia.

The military dictators could play any game but democratically elected representatives from Thailand and Indonesia recognize the importance of working together in close harmony with each other and foster friendly relations between their respective countries. The future looks bright and promising.

U.S Thai-relations

While laying out a frame work for U.S Thai foreign policy, the following criteria should be considered. Number one: What level of closeness the existing relations exist between the two countries? Number two: What should be the U.S policy, anticipating the rise of Chinese influence in South East Asia; both of these questions have to be looked into closely.

The present relations between Thailand and United States are friendly, cordial and close. United States can count on Thailand just as it can with Japan, Australia and South Korea. However, there are certain fine prints to read between these relations. South Korea and Japan are proven allies. Thailand, on the other hand can not be taken for granted. It has established very solid friendly relations with China. In other words, Thailand would weigh its position very seriously in case of any kind of conflict that might come up in future between China and the United States. It will not just dump its friendship with China which it has built for a number of years. China is a next door neighbor; U.S.A is a distant far off land. There is a large Chinese local community living in Thailand. These are some important considerations that do play significant role in making some decisions. Thailand is not a protégé of China; it is realizing the powerful influence of China in global politics and wants to have the best leverage out of the two worlds. For United States to change this position, it has to take some dramatic steps in its diplomacy towards Thailand.

The political gurus in Washington have to evaluate how much attention it should bestow on Bangkok. There are other destinations too like Jakarta, Manila or KaualaLumpur. They have to pick up those locations which could pay the highest dividends. Naturally, it will depend upon the resources that United States is going to put up to achieve its goals. Looking from many logistical reasoning, Jakarta may present a good case but not at the expense of Bangkok.

Thailand could never be controlled by China; it is the only country where the Communist party is outlawed. Religion plays a very dominant part in the daily live of a Thailand citizen. Communist China's ideologies would not fly in this country. There are two strategies before the United States policy makers namely Incremental Enhancement or Quantum Move. It will mean taking a chance on getting what you want for sure or what would you like to happen in due course. It seems, at this moment that Thailand would walk on a course of a balanced trajectory. It may not take the United States dictate all the time and follow an independent policy which might favor China.

This is however clear that Thailand is a valuable ally that could prove highly beneficial in time of critical need. United States should continue to expand its assistance in different areas including military build up and advanced technical education and public health. Thailand needs more engineers and business executives and better health facilities and good infra structure to give it a big boost. United States can provide all of these to gain long lasting friendship from Thailand. This may be in the best interest of the United States too. Thailand is not tarnished in public corruption as other Asian countries are and that is a big plus. Thai Monarchy is a big stable force in the country. People are friendly and militants do not make news in the country; it is a big difference to think about

PHILIPPINES

It is a country of seven thousand islands; only eleven of them are suitable for living. There are active volcanoes and lot of mountains; flat land is not plentiful. It has endured colonialism for almost three hundred years from Spanish rulers and after the defeat of Spain in U.S Spanish War in 1998 it became a colony of the United States. Philippines gained its independence in 1946.

The country is facing lot of problems on many fronts. It has one of the highest population growths in the world. The present population is ninety   three millions and it is estimated that it will be doubled in three decades. One third of the population lives below poverty levels-less than a dollar a day. Public corruption is present every where. Ex Presidents Marcos and   Estrada are notable examples of this widely spread corruption circle. A   significant percentage of government revenues, almost six percent, come from the remittances of foreign expatriates. Unemployment is high and people do not see a bright future for them under the present conditions.

The present President of Philippines is Benigno Noynoy Aquino, son of former President Cory Aquino. In his election campaigns he said" I will no only not steal but I will run after thieves. When there is no corruption there is no poverty". Noynoy does not have any political experience and faces uphill tasks; it is not only to reduce corruption, improve economical conditions but also to fight Muslim militants and Communists radicals. Would he succeed, time will show.

Where ever there is poverty and there are no outlets to make a living, sex industry starts its roots. Like in Thailand, Philippines has a thriving sex industry. It is said forty percent of tourists visit Philippines to satisfy their sex cravings. It is unfortunate but some what true.

Most of the developing countries of Asia and Africa have fallen prey to this wide spread disease of corruption all over the society. The result in all these cases has been disastrous to the people who had to endure this crime and face tremendous difficulties in their daily lives. In Philippines, they say People Power has thrown out two Presidents from power; it is true. However, the country has not been able to produce a good, efficient and sustainable governing body that could change the present pathetic conditions that are prevailing in the country.

What should be the role of the United States under the present conditions? It is a very good question. Philippines is a reliable and a solid ally just like Japan and South Korea. It is in the interest of the United States to see Philippines as a prosperous and strong partner in the global political arena. In 1991, United States abandoned its Clark Air Base and these militants; the progress is not spectacular, however.

To take a good tangential take off for industrialization, any country has to improve its transport structure-roads, railways, shipping ports and airports facilities. Attractive tax incentives for foreign investments are essential for developing countries. Favorable Government policies, Taxes, Import/Export duties and regulated fair business practices are very important factors to move forward in the direction of rapid industrialization. The Philippines government has to look into its practices and policies to keep it in touch with the changing times, on a regular basis. there are no military personnel stationed in Philippines on a permanent basis at this present juncture. It does lead to important questions.

Local Conditions

Progress made by any country depends upon many factors. China started Special Economic Zones (SEZ) and changed the entire structure of the country. From a very poor rural economy, it became a highly vibrant and successful industrialized nation. Thirty million people came out of dire poverty and joined the middle class. The concept behind these Economic Zones was based upon two important factors; first the government gave full support to establish new production facilities and secondly it encouraged the enterprising business community to start a business at favorable conditions. And it worked very well.

It shows that the top leadership along with its supporting governing structure created an environment that could be converted into profitable business organizations. This condition can be transformed into a viable situation only if there were energetic, entrepreneurial group of people to make it happen. These people have to have some good idea of running a business. The prerequisites of Capital and Business Knowledge should be there to make it a success story. The Chinese model met these requirements squarely.

If we look at Philippines from this perspective, we immediately realize that both of these factors are missing partially or completely from the scene. When the corruption is rampant from top to the bottom and there are not many people to take chance or not equipped to run the business, then the model would not work. People in Philippines do not see bright future ahead of them and therefore they are migrating to other countries for a better life. There are three million Filipinos in the United States, one million in Saudi Arabia; altogether eleven millions who have said good bye to their own country. It is estimated that the money sent by these expatriates is more than the foreign direct investment in the country. This is not a good condition for any country whether it is Philippines or Greece. People will always migrate to other countries wherever there are better opportunities but a progressive country has to have a core conducting climate where business could thrive well. It is the government and the people who form the core; to take the country forward.

Philippines is facing a serious problem in Mindanao island, in the south where Muslim Separatist Groups are staging terrorist activities against the government and the general public. At the request of the Philippines government, United States military personnel are helping the Philippines army units to drive out

When we compare other developing countries of Pacific and South East Asia like Malaysia, Thailand and Indonesia, Philippines stands at the bottom ladder. Strong leadership and support from the people can change this position.

Philippines and ASEAN

Association of South East Asian Nations (ASEAN) consisting of Philippines, Indonesia, Malaysia, Thailand, Viet Nam, Laos, Cambodia and Burma has been enlarged now to have, China, India, Australia and Japan as observers. The association has helped the member countries to forge Free Trade Agreements between them and establish closer social, cultural and security relations. The goal and objectives of ASEAN is to duplicate the structure of the European Union (EU) in Asia.

Philippines is an active member of ASEAN as well as of Association of Pacific Economic Cooperation (APEC). It is the most important Non NATO ally of the United States. The foreign policy of Philippines has consistently supported the United States stand globally. Let us look at some of the countries.

Japan: During World War II, Philippines was occupied by the Imperialist Japanese Army. About a million Philippines died fighting the Japanese occupation. After 1946, when Philippines became an independent country, cordial and friendly relations were established between Japan and Philippines. And at this juncture, Japan is number one source of foreign investment in the country. It is estimated that Philippines has the second largest reserves of gold and copper in the world, besides other commodities. However, they are untapped. Stability, transparency in governance, infrastructure, education standard, technical know how and favorable business environment are some of the prerequisites for attracting foreign capital in the country. For some reason or the other, the Philippines has not succeeded in this direction.

China: It is interesting to note that Philippines did not recognize the Communist Government in Beijing as the legitimate representative of China till 1975; it was the Nationalist Government of Taiwan that was recognized as the official government of mainland China. Now, Philippines follow the same policy towards Taiwan as the United States does and that is "One China policy, and no forceful annexation of Taiwan by Beijing government." Philippines could follow this policy because it had the full backing of the United States. China and Philippines along with other countries like Viet Nam, Malaysia and Japan have differences over the sovereignty of oil and gas rich islands located in the South China Sea. According to Chinese, these islands belong to China; other countries do not agree with this. China has signed a Free Trade Agreement with Philippines with the result that the two way trade figures have ballooned to four billion dollars in 2010. It is an impressive improvement from the past. Philippines and China are chugging along on good terms. As long as Philippines has the security umbrella from the United States, China would like to keep friendly relations with Philippines. This trend would follow in the future.

India: Relations between Philippines and India are friendly .Indian Prime-Minister Dr.Man Mohan Singh visited Philippines and Gloria Arroyo, President of Philippines came to India to promote trade and economical cooperation. A target of two way business transactions was set at one billion dollars for 2010. This figure is very small given the huge opportunities that these two countries can carve out. Philippines Service and manufacturing organizations can use Indian I.T.T expertise at a fraction of cost compared to the United States.

U.S-Philippines Relations

United States and Philippines have established close relations starting from 1954 when SEATO-South East Asia Treaty Organization-was formed. At the present juncture, both of these countries can count on each other. In other words they need each other for their own security, welfare and influence. Starting from the thorny issue of Taiwan U.S.A has agreed on one China policy on the condition that mainland China would not use force to annex Taiwan. Philippines has adopted the same policy; it did not recognize the Communist government till 1975. There is an influential Chinese community in Philippines which has strong connections with the Taiwan Nationalist Party which had fought against Mao .In case China decides to use force against Taiwan, at any future date, United States can bank on the support of Philippines without any reservation. It is a big plus in these complex political situations.

It is a well known fact that at some distant future, China would confront the supremacy of the United States in Pacific Asia and else where. Right now, China is laying its claim on oil and gas rich islands located in South China Sea. Many other Asian countries namely Viet Nam and Malaysia dispute this claim. Furthermore, Chinese navy ships are sending signals that United States does not have full freedom to go around China's coast line. China is telling other Asian countries that they have to deal with it rather than the United States to have the freedom of navigation around China Seas. United States has a powerful Navy which China would not dare to confront with. At the same time, it can create some kind of trouble which could escalate into some dangerous situation. United States needs some reliable regional allies to face this possibility.

After 9/11 many countries are facing problems from Muslim militants. They want to create strict, conservative religious empires throughout the world which would enforce Sharias laws and fanatical ways of living. Philippines is going through this situation in Mindanao island, in the south. At the request of the Philippines government, United States specially trained military personnel are helping the Philippines army units to fight this Al Queada supported recruits. United States knows very well that these terrorists could cause lot of damage as we see in Afghanistan, Pakistan and else where.

Philippines economy is not robust and it needs support. United States is providing assistance in the areas of education, public health, agriculture and military training. Some how, things are not moving fast mainly because of rampant corruption starting from the top to the bottom as well as exploding population and absence of essential business structure-ethics and controls. From the United States point of view, it is very important to have reliable allies. If it requires more resources to spend, it would be worth while because the stakes are high. China's threat is real and it will not be a passing phase. In order to maintain the Super power status, United States has to go a step further to achieve its goal. In the long run, China, India and the United States would be the leading contenders of influence in that part of Asia. It is better to be ready and prepare for the worse scenario in the global political stage. United States foreign policy should start charting out its plan of actions, from this point of view. The long range planning should be to elevate Philippines socio-political structure.

AUSTRALIA

It is one of the tenth richest countries of the world with a gross national income around thirty eight thousand dollars. Interestingly to note how a colony of convicts transformed itself into this startling stature of wealth and prosperity. It was 1770, when Captain James Cook of England landed his ship near Sydney harbor and laid foundation for this country. From White Australia of Sixties, it became a nation of many nationalities from Asia, Europe and England .The present generation of Australia is multi cultural and forward looking.

The previous governments of Australia considered themselves as European and British; somehow forced to live in the Asian continent. Gradually, it started dawning on their thinking that it is in their own interest to consider themselves as part of Asian community and build friendly relations with them. The largest trading partners of Australia are Japan, China and South Korea and not England and Germany. It has now established not only commercial and business treaties with these countries but it has military and security related agreements with Japan, South Korea and Philippines.

Australia is endowed with national resources of all kinds; there is plenty of coal, iron, aluminum, uranium and liquid petroleum gas. All of these commodities are in high demand. In 2009, China signed an agreement with Exxon Mobil of Australia worth 50 billions for Liquid Petroleum Products. Australia is the largest exporter of wool; it has plenty of wheat and meat to satisfy the hunger of the world. Beside these natural resources, Australia's second largest foreign exchange earner is College degrees. More than 90,000 students come from China and India and thousands come from South Korea and other countries. The Australian Universities have established themselves well in the education world.

The role of Australia in world politics is not prominent; with a population around twenty millions but plenty of living land-as big as the United States, it has the potential of a great power. The negative aspects are that it does not have a large standing army and does not command a big Air force or Navy. Economically, it is in a strong position-has more than two trillion Gross Domestic Product; however, on military grounds it is far behind China, India and even Pakistan. Economics as well as Military strength are the two leading indicators which define the power of any nation. Australia is just not there. There are some Think Tanks who proposed some radical ideas to attain that high position in world politics. Kevin Rudd, Prime-Minister of Australia presented some of his thoughts as to how Australia could become a great power by opening wide the gates of immigration from Asia and some European countries. It is very true that large scale of immigration to the United States in the last century and after words did become a pivotal point in moving the country to its glorious glory. Immigrants have made U.S.A what it is today-a Super Power.

Local Scene

Australia now has the first female Prime-Minister-Julia Gillard. She was an assistant to the former Prime-Minister Kevin Rudd. Kevin had lost the support of his party and Gillard took over. Only time will show how successful she would be; Australians are watching.

With all the fanfare and tight security, fifty four countries of the Commonwealth are meeting in Perth-Oct'2011.Australia and Canada are the two most important members of this organization. All these years, the organization of the Commonwealth has not acted decisively and coherently within itself or globally. Two billion people belong to this organization with almost one third of Global Gross Domestic Product. Lack of available funds and shortage of directed efforts are perhaps the main reasons for this organization for not playing its role effectively. Walk your Talk is the slogan that has been heard for this organization.

Off and on, political parties bring out the question of Australia becoming a republic, discarding the queen of England as the head of Australian government. It seems that the majority is in favor of keeping the queen. More than seventy percent of Australians have British connections and people like the queen. That settles the question.

People of Chinese origin had settled down in Australia long time ago; every large city in Australia has a China town. It is said that about three percent of Australian population would have people of Asian origin in 2015.There is a small minority of Japanese, Koreans as well as Indians. In 2007, some white racists had started hate campaigns against Indians and many Indian students were murdered in Melbourne. The local police authority did not do their job well; Australian-Indian government relations had reached the breaking point .But now, the situation is supposedly under control.

As mentioned before, Australia is a rich country with all kinds of natural resources. Furthermore, it has established itself as a good source of providing college education. Instead of going to U.S.A or England, many Asian students now go to Australian Universities. However, it is interesting to note that Australia has not developed a booming manufacturing industry in any area nor does it have the modern Software industry. The same comment is true in case of Service industry. Australian companies have not hit the global markets with the exception of commercial communications where Mr.Murdoch is the king.

Depending upon the leadership of Australia, its vision and its actions, the country could either stay in the same incremental progressive mode or choose to take off on a dramatic high influential trajectory. Kevin Rudd had expounded his thoughts on this topic .To go with his ideas Australia had to bring about many socio-economical changes.

Relations with other countries

China is one of the most important countries in terms of trade-import and export transactions for Australia. China needs coal, iron, uranium, liquid petroleum gas and other commodities for its industries which Australia can provide without any problem. Very recently, there were some troubles between Chinese government and Australia over a mining company and that made the Prime-Minister of Australia Kevin Rudd speak out loudly, saying that relations with China are not always easy to maintain. In 2007, Prime-Minister John Howard met Dalai Lama ; that brought angry protests from the Chinese. Kevin Rudd who speaks fluent Mandarin raised the question of Tibet and human rights with the Chinese Prime-Minister in 2009; the Chinese government did not like this discussion, at all. The Australian officials can talk to the Chinese boldly because they have the assurance of the United States, in the background. Interestingly, it is Australia that has a positive trading balance with China unlike United States. China and Australia are moving along fine in business area; however, China knows very well where Australia stands in world politics. It can be said without any hesitation that in case the Taiwan problem comes up, Australia along with Japan, would stand behind the United States.

Japan and South Korea: Japan and South Korea are the leading investor resources for Australia. Business is booming between these three countries. Japan and Korea needs Australian wheat, meat, liquid petroleum gas and uranium for their industries. Japan and South Korea are the largest suppliers of electronic goods, automobiles, appliances and other daily living products to Australia. All these three countries are aligned with the United States on military basis and are considered as reliable allies. Japan, Australia and South Korea are strong economically and can exert tremendous clout in global politics.

Indonesia: With a population around 240 million strong, Indonesia is the third largest democracy in the world. It is a moderate Muslim country. However, isolated anti-western Muslim groups do raise their flags and cause trouble in the country off and on. Back in 2002, a militant group planted bombs in a restaurant in the island of Bali where most of the customers are foreigners; more than two hundred Australians were killed in that explosion. Unlike Pakistan where the majority of the population is against Americans, a local Indonesian is not anti-American or anti-west. The present President of Indonesia, Susilo Yudhoyono wants to establish close relationship with the United States and with Australia. In 2007, Australia and Indonesia had some rough relations on account of East Timor freedom movement. Australia had supported East Timor independence from Indonesia; later on, Australia and Indonesia joined hands and East Timor became an independent country.

India: Relations with India are not the friendliest; numerous murders of innocent Indian students in Melbourne in 2007 do not speak very well of the Australian authorities, specially the local police. There are some white racist elements in Australia that are still living in the cages of ignorance and hatred. India was outraged so much that at one point in time the break up of diplomatic relations was a possibility. When these obnoxious people are not booked for indulging in these kinds of nefarious activities, it becomes a matter of shame.

India and Australia can become good partners provided some new ideas and enthusiasm from both countries are put in place. India does not need coal, iron, meat, wheat, wool and other commodities from Australia. However, Liquid Petroleum Gas and Uranium are needed by India. Australia on the other hand can benefit from Indian Software companies. Relations between these two countries could chug along smoothly provided there is some real understanding and appreciation of each others culture and point of views. If Australia wants to take some visionary steps to propel itself as a great power, it has to seek Indian and Chinese immigrants to take it there.

Australia-U.S Relations

United States and Australia have worked very closely with each other just like Japan and the United Kingdom. Australians have supported the United States in Korea, Viet Nam, Afghanistan and Iraqi war. From military and economic point of view, these two countries are linked with each other through ANZUS (Australia, New Zealand and United States) and APEC (Association of Pacific Economic Cooperation) and Free Trade Association. United States is the largest investor in Australia; it holds second and fourth places in terms of imports and exports. Leaders of both countries have paid regular visits to each other country. Prime-Minister Julia Gillard paid a visit to the United States in 2011.PresidentBush and other American officials have gone to Australia and reaffirmed their friendship and cooperation in world political arena.

Though Australia is one of the richest countries of the world, yet it can not be counted as a military power. China, India and Pakistan are far ahead in this game. In case of any conflict in Asia, Australia will support the United States, without any reservation. The question is how affective that support would be. There are three nuclear powers sitting in Asia; they carry more weight than Australia. The foreign policy of the United States should explore thoroughly the ways and means of building a stronger Australia, from the military point of view. It will be in interest of the United States to move in this direction.

Since Australia has the security umbrella from the United States, why should it spend precious resources in building a big military machine? To some it does not make any sense but to others it is a different story. Time and circumstances would play a big part in deciding what would be the best for Australia.

United States could encourage the Australian government to provide economical, educational, health care, agricultural and other kinds of assistance to less developed Asian countries like Indonesia, Thailand, Viet Nam, Sri Lanka and others which would ultimately provide wealth and prosperity to the region.

Poverty, ignorance and frustration are the main reason for all this terrorist activity which is raging in Afghanistan, Pakistan, Iraq and else where. Well to do countries like Australia can make a big difference along with the help from the United State .As we see today, Australia and the United States would continue to be good friends and would help each other in any conflict or need. Both countries realize the benefits of walking on the same lane. United States need many friendly countries to keep its position as a Super Power.

SOUTH KOREA

One of the most dynamic countries of Asia is Republic of Korea; proclaimed an independent country in 1948. The population of South Korea is around fifty millions; the Gross National Income is $20,000 per capita. It is 12th largest economy of the world.

North Korea invaded South Korea in 1950 and finally the war ended in 1953 with 38th parallel as a dividing line between the two countries. There are about 38,000 American military personnel stationed in South Korea to safeguard the security of the country against the North Koreans.

South Korea was governed by military generals for four decades and only in 1993, the first civilian president was elected to the highest office. High corruption and authoritarian rule was the prevailing norm in the country; at the same time the government was encouraging family owned businesses called Chaebol. Samsung and Hyundai family of companies were prominent then and later on, they became the global companies. The present President of South Korea Lee Myung-bak was the Chief Executive Officer of Hyundai before he was elected as President in 2008.

South Korea is a thriving democracy at this juncture. It is one of those countries where high speed –broad band-and wireless internet service is used by the majority of the people. South Korea has become famous for its electronic and automotive products throughout the world. It has earned its reputation as the roaring giant of Pacific Asia.

If we look towards East Asia, three countries stand out as the most reliable allies of the United States. They are South Korea, Japan and Australia. The imminent danger to U.S supremacy in that part of the world is China's growing influence. As things stand today, United States would not find India as an adversary in the near future or even in the long run. India could become as close as South Korea and Japan are, depending upon prevailing circumstances. The foreign policies of the United States have to consider different aspects as to zero in where to pay the most attention to form a solid group of allies.

The differences between North and South Korea are as wide as Sunshine and night darkness, from all aspects of daily living and governance. There were some discussions of reunion of North and South Korea during 1998-2000. President Kim Dae-jung of South Korea proposed a policy of cooperation and conciliation towards North Korea; he called it Sun Shine Policy. This policy was aimed to provide food, oil, fertilizer and other basic commodities to the people of North Korea to save thousand of people from starvation and death. This policy was a friendly gesture from South Korea to assure North Korea that it wants to end all kinds of hostility and begin an era of peaceful coexistence. At the same time, it was understood that North Korea would abandon its ambition of becoming a nuclear power. President Kim was awarded the Nobel Prize for Peace for his Sun Shine Policy. But North Korea did not give up its plans.

Relations with North Korea
It was President Bush who called North Korean government as Axis of Evil; Iran and Iraq were the other two countries which formed this group. All these countries were governed by dictators and thousand of people were killed under their brutal regimes. Saddam of Iraq has gone but North Korean and Iranian dictators are still in power. It is not easy to dislodge dictators; it is tough to deal with them because they are cunning and manipulators. They govern the people through brute force and want to show that they are the supreme power. It is very difficult for the ordinary citizen to rise against such merciless and egoistic persons. It is unfortunate that South Korea has to face such a situation. It is South Korea which has to take the major damage in case the dictatorial ruler of North Korea decides to start a war against the south.

The present President of South Korea LeeMyung-bak is a hard liner and he ended the Sun Shine policy towards North Korea. He made it clear to the North Korean government that unless it abandons its nuclear program, South Korea would not provide financial and other humanitarian assistance to the North. In retaliation, North Korea attacked a South Korean naval ship; about forty six sailors died. Again in Nov 2010, North Korea started a border war. It created a tense situation. United States and South Korea in response staged a joint military exercise on the sea to send the message that such activities would not be tolerated and force would be used to repulse these attacks.

At this juncture, United States and South Korea are asking China, Russia and Japan to put pressure on the North Korean government to come to a peaceful settlement with the South; meaning that it has to give up its nuclear program. The question is: will the South Korean government succeed in its efforts? The North Korean government wants a guarantee from the United States that it would not be attacked; furthermore, it wants United States to withdraw the American military personnel from South Korea. Under the present circumstances, it would be difficult for the United States to agree to these two conditions knowing the changing moods and attitudes of the North Koreans. It seems that North Korea, in this scenario would not budge from its position of continuing its nuclear program and this impasse would continue to linger on.

The political observers have said that neither China nor Russia wants North Korea to become a nuclear power because they are not sure how the dictators of North Korea would react after they acquired the nuclear weapons. At the same token, it is a sure bet that both of these countries would oppose an attack on the nuclear facilities of the North, by the United States, South Korea and other western countries. It is imperative, therefore to devise a consensus between the North Koreans and the United Nations to resolve this thorny situation. A broad policy of engagement and containment has to be drawn which should meet at the middle of the road. Sun Shine policy but no appeasement would be a way to go.

Since North Korea has come along to this stage where they can produce nuclear weapons in large quantities in the near future, it seems that it would not give up its nuclear program-they may not proceed openly but they would do it secretly to avoid opposition from different parts of the world. Once they have reached that stage, they might start talking and show to the world their power.

United States and South Korea
The closet allies of the United States in East Asia are Japan, Australia and South Korea. The hot spots for trouble are Taiwan and North Korea. South Korea can not stand on its own feet as far as national security is concerned. The dark looming clouds of North Korean nuclear threats are present all the time. Mass starvation, deprivation and political oppression in North Korea, is a constant destabilizing factor for South Korean government. A relatively well off South Korea has to face a nuclear, dictatorial and poor neighbor, North Korea, every day of the year.

North Korea is almost a nuclear state and at top of it, has large army to march into South Korea. United States has to maintain a sizeable military force in South Korea to deflect the North Korean potential threats. North Korea would continue to play petty games of provocation as to divert some attention from its secret nuclear program as well as make its case strong for financial and food aid.

United States has to adopt a multi directed policy of Containment and Engagement. Among Russia, Japan and China, the most influential country to bend or change North Korean policies, is China. It is the only country which can provide good financial support as well as humanitarian aid. Japan and Russia are not in a position to extend any significant assistance to North Korea. United States has to work with China to keep North Korea in line. After earthquake and tsunami disaster in Japan in March 2011, Japan can not afford to provide financial help to North Korea. Looking from Chinese point of view, it does not want to see a nuclear power in its backyard. This line of thinking would evolve into a favorable response to the United States and South Korea.

As far as Containment policies are concerned, some sanctions from United Nations would be necessary. Export of military hardware like missiles and similar items to Middle East countries or Africa has to be strictly checked through the channels of United Nations and United States Navy. The idea is to siphon off the monetary gains and deprive the North Korean regime of foreign funds. Shortage of available funds would delay the success of the North Korean nuclear program. At the same time, International Atomic Energy Agency (IAEA) has to keep an eye on nuclear operations of North Korea.

The policy of no appeasement, no provocation might prove to be a winner. United States would not be able to stop the nuclear program of North Korea unless it goes out all the way to demolish the nuclear facilities. However, it could surely delay its progress. Down the road, North Korea might start thinking in other directions. Change of leadership, change in national priorities and other factors could come into picture and a so called rogue state may turn out to be different.

The North Korean government may genuinely think that a movement for reunion of two Koreas may gather momentum in the near future if the ordinary citizen in the North remains in poverty and oppression and at the same time the South keeps on moving forward in a big way in terms of prosperity, security and higher standard of living. The dictators of the North would not like this situation. They would not like to abdicate their power; in fact, reunion of the two into a single country like Germany, would not be in their own self interest. They would not give away their crown. The chances of reunion of North and South are out of sight; the two countries are so apart, economically.

What if Scenarios: American Strategies

Consider the case when North Korea does become a Nuclear Power. How South Korea would react, how the United States would alert itself to this situation and how China and Russia would embrace this change-it would be an interestingly important scenario to reflect upon.

The immediate affect of this changed situation would be felt by South Korea; an impoverished nuclear country governed by dictators could become a big de stabilizer to an affluent democratic modern country. Without the military help from the United States, South Korea could be run over by the North Koreans, once again. The presence of the American forces is a must for security and stability of South Korea. The intention of North Korean leaders is to become a nuclear power whatever time frame it takes. At that moment in history, it would be in good leverage position to extract as much monetary and other benefits from the United States and South Korea.

There are some robust and turning point strategies available to the United States and South Korea that could change the course of action of the North Koreans. A non aggression pact with North Korea as proposed by the North Koreans with the United States might signal a positive assurance to that country. As long as North Korea maintains a friendly posture towards the South, the non aggression pact could become a turning point. The other important strategy would be to continue the Sun Shine Policy towards the North. Citizens of North Korea need help. Financial and food problems have to be addressed by the United States and South Korea. Further more, a Containment Policy restricting the progress of nuclear program has to be kept in place. This three pronged strategic policy could sprout the seeds of co operation and mutual trust between the United States and North Korea.

The two most important allies of North Korea are China and Russia. It is a sure bet that nether of these two countries want to see North Korea becoming a nuclear power. The mature leadership of Russia and China would not trust the new leaders of North Korea. The arrogant and ego maniac leaders from North Korea could create problems not only for South Korea but for the whole world. Only China is in a position to provide monetary and other transformational help to North Korea; Russia does not have that clout. The United States has to take help from China; however, it might be pointed out that China might not be agreeing to the point of view of the United States.

Since 2009, no progress has been made in negotiations with the North Koreans. To take a turning point decision, the United States and South Korea have to take unilateral steps and forget China and Russia; otherwise, it will continue to drag on. It will be a big advantage for North Korea to buy more time for developing its nuclear program. North Korea and Iran have similar objectives; both of these countries are very near to their targets. Applying sanctions and other political pressures will not deter them from moving forward in their quest to have nuclear weapons.

South Korea-A strong ally

The world is changing fast. New global powers are emerging. Asia is attracting center of attention. China and India are replacing European influence. At this moment in history, the United States is the only Super power in terms of financial and military strength. But Super powers too, need reliable and consistent allies. In Pacific Asia, United States has only three countries that could be counted as solid partners. They are: Japan, Australia and South Korea. All these countries have supported the United States from time to time and this trend seems likely to continue in future.

China is going to compete against the United States in global political arena just as Russia did in the past. From the military point of view, China is far behind the United States but in the coming decades things might change. In South East Asia, India is the only country that could stand side by side with America and could counter the weight of China. Given the financial strength of the South Korean economy and military support from the United States, South Korea could be counted as a solid partner of the United States. If China becomes a threat to the United States in Asia, it is a possibility that Japan might change its military policy and once again become a military power to balance the Chinese influence.

At present, South Korea has the largest business relations with China, Japan and the United States and this trading volume will continue to expand. South Korea would not like to see Chinese influence spread on the trading routes and would support the United States in its endeavor to keep its influence. If things go well with the South Korean economy, it might jump into sixth or seventh world economy. In other words, South Korea would be an asset to the United States; a country to rely upon. If there is a conflict between Taiwan and China, will South Korea oppose China? It is a difficult question to answer at this stage. Under the present conditions, United States is bound to support Taiwan and following the lead of the United States, South Korea might throw its weight in favor of the Taiwanese people.

Though Philippine is a supporter of the United States, but its economy is weak and South Korea is much advanced in all aspects of structural stability. Indonesia is another country which could side with America. The present President of Indonesia wants the United States to help the country in terms of investment and other kinds of assistance. The strategic political planners of the United States should count on countries which profess to side with U.S presently and are not cozy with Russia and China.

In the next decade or two, South Korea would move progressively towards higher Gross Domestic Product and greater national income. United States should take steps to strengthen further economic and military ties with South Korea. South Korea has a thriving democracy and making important inroads for spreading prosperity throughout the region. It will be South Korea that could, in partnership with the United States, transform the aggressive designs of North Korea.

JAPAN

The third largest economy in the world is Japan; China has taken the second position now. Japan, Australia and Singapore have the highest standard of living in East Asia. The gross national income per capita is around 40k. The population recorded in year 2010 is 127 millions. It is a homogenous society. More than seventy percent of people live in urban areas. Shintoism, Buddhism and Christianity are the main religion of the people. In 1947, a new constitution was written; absolute monarchy was abolished and the country has a thriving democratic set up. According to the new constitution, Japan does not have the freedom of having a full fledged army, navy or land forces. United States keeps around 40,000 military personnel in Okinawa and guarantees the safety of Japan against foreign attack. After World War II, Japan has become one of the most loyal partners of the United States.

Japan has built a society of highly trained and educated citizens. During 1950 to 1990, Japan became the work shop of the world. Automobiles and electronic goods were sold through out the globe. In 1997, Japan fell into a deep recession and financial crisis changed the whole picture. The Gross Domestic Product has taken a steep fall.

In March 2011, severe earth quake hit Japan; tsunami waves swept away hundred of homes and thousands of people perished. Three nuclear reactors located in Fukushima caught fire and finally they have to be shut down for good. Japan economy suffered a devastating blow; many production facilities were closed. It will require billions of dollars to bring back the normal conditions. Thousand of people are living in temporary shelters; fishing industry has suffered a serious set back. Under this calamity, Japanese people have shown great courage and determination to stand on their feet again.

This natural disaster in Japan had repercussions not only in Japan but it has affected many other countries in Asia. Japan has been a source of investment and financial assistance to Asian countries and now it has to spend billions of dollars in its own country. It means this reservoir of investment and economic aid has disappeared at least for few years.

The keen competition in this age requires many capabilities and collaboration among the top global companies. Japan, Germany, England, France, United States and South Korea are the leading countries where innovation and new businesses are bringing more prosperity and efficiency to the whole world. Japan has established itself as the leading most producer of electronic products and automobiles. To keep this momentum going on strong, lot of money has to be spent on Research and Development. Sharp business judgment would play a key role in taking the top position in the industry. In the past, Japan has done a good job in maintaining its superior position. However, Korean and Chinese companies are coming up fast in bringing new ideas and processes to cut down cost of production and at the same time producing quality products. No country or company has monopoly on any area of business activity. It is an open field. The success would depend upon agility, new ideas and different avenues of marketing. Software and mobility would play important role in driving the desired results. Japan has not shown good progress in software innovation.

Japan's recent past

Japan like Germany wanted to dominate over its neighbors. In 1937, it attacked China and about 300,000 civilian Chinese were ruthlessly killed in what is called the Rape of Nanjing. During 1939-40, Japan occupied French Indo-China-Vietnam, Cambodia and Laos. And in 1941, Japan mounted a surprise devastating attack on Pearl Harbor. Since 1932, Japan military generals were the dictating force in the country. Japan saw the end of its supremacy when it surrendered in August 1945, thus ending the World War II.

The new constitution written in 1947, established a new era of social and cultural transformation. The king was no more a divine god. However, some of the structural strata of the Japanese society-thinking, mixing with other nationalities-still remained in force. A dormant feeling of racial superiority still persists in certain sections of the Japanese society. During the last sixty years, Japan has seen tremendous changes and in East Asia, Japan is one of the most westernized countries in the world.

Japan signed a Peace Treaty with the United States in 1951. Under this treaty United States guarantee the safety against any military attack on the country. At the same time, Japan does not have the luxury of becoming a full fledged military force-a condition similar to Germanys surrender. The history of Germany and Japan shows common threads. Though the times have changed, yet in the future nobody can say that there are no chances of having another

Hitler or Hiro Hito, in these two countries. The world community has to have safeguards against any future catastrophe and global turmoil.

The countries of Asia do not want to see a military giant in Japan; just as they do not want China to take its place. At the present moment, many countries of Asia have started feeling the disguised danger of Chinese threat. In a situation like this, United States has to outline its strategic policies so that it could minimize the Chinese threat and at the same time keep Japan becoming a military power. In order to maintain the Super Power status, United States has to keep the upper edge in terms of its military power as well as its economic supremacy. The importance of having reliable allies is the key factor here. Australia and India can play very important role in this geo politics.

China and South Korea are the leading trading partners of Japan, at present. Both of these countries were subjugated by Japan and some historical animosities still linger on. Formal apologies from Japanese leaders for the past mistakes in history are not considered adequate by the Chinese and Korean public. Japan has to show its openness and overcome the barriers of integration not only with Chinese and Koreans but with the rest of the world.

The third largest economy of the world stands on highly educated, technically smart and sharp business talented Japanese people. The past history is surrounded with the aura of courage and ancestral superiority. The recent past tells the story of a western oriented, efficient democratic country. It is a reliable ally of the United States. Its relations with Russia and China are not cozy. However, there are good chances of building strategic relations with South Korea, India and Australia. Its influence on North Korea is minimal.

U.S-Japan relations

At the present moment, U.S-Japan relations are standing tall. Japan had supported the United States against Saddam Husain in Kuwaiti war; it supported President Bush in Iraq and in Afghanistan. The two countries have no conflicting interests in global politics. However, there are certain areas where the two countries do not agree.

Right now, Japan is raising the question of sovereignty of certain islands in Pacific Asia against Russian claim; it might be interesting to know that Japan was the first Asian country to defeat a European nation and that was Russia. There are some oil and gas rich islands in China Sea where many countries including Malaysia, China and Japan are claiming the right of ownership. Where the U.S would stand in these minor conflicts, it is not defined as of now.

The most disturbing and potentially explosive situation of Taiwan's independence would test the Japanese collaboration with the United States. If mainland China attacks Taiwan, United States most probably would warn China to retreat. Russia in such a situation would favor China. Japan and Australia would consider their position and India would not get involved at all.

Consider the case of Iran. Japan needs oil from Iranians. United States and Iran are not on the same table. President Bush called Iran an evil empire. Can Japan afford to ignore Iran or cut off relations? Japan and the United States, in this case, may not agree with each other. There was a time when Japan was basking in huge surpluses in international trade with the United States and with many other countries of the world. It was the same situation as we are seeing today with China. United States had to tell Japan that this situation is not warranted and some actions have to be taken. Just like the present day Chinese currency, Yen was undervalued against the dollar. The American government did not agree with the Japanese and those were highly critical disagreements between the two countries.

There are two very crucial questions that have to be addressed. The number one question is: Would the United States allow the Japanese government to become a strong military power once again, considering the background of Chinese aggressive posturing in Asia? The second important question is: Will the American military personnel stationed in Okinawa and elsewhere be gradually withdrawn? To answer these two questions in categorical terms is difficult. We have to go back to Japanese history: Japan had been an imperial empire and since 1920 it has built a picture of an aggressor country until 1945 when it lost the war against the American forces. Just like Germany, Japan has to build trust amongst the community of nations that history would not be repeated in the future. Germany and Japan have inflicted irreparable damage to the well being and prosperity of the world in the past and it is difficult to forget.

In the interest of world peace, it would be advisable that both countries-Japan and Germany should never be given freedom to become a military force. It does not mean that they should look to the United States to defend them. They should be capable to defend themselves with out the aid of other countries. The world cannot afford to have a World War III. Safeguards have to be in place to avoid such a possibility. This perspective should be the guiding principle for U.S.A.

Japan, United States and South East Asia

At the present point in history, United States and Japan have forged solid relationship of fraternity and mutually beneficial common goals. What is good for America in global political arena is supposedly good for Japan. Both of these countries have doubts and suspicions about Chinese intentions in South East Asia. For United States to maintain its supremacy in this region, it is imperative that it should establish long term friendship with countries like Thailand, Indonesia, Vietnam and Philippines. We are assuming that Australia and the United States would continue to be good allies, now and in future.

For these countries in South East Asia to be friendly with the United States and Japan, some kind of incentives in terms of financial assistance and other programs related to education, healthcare and social interactions, have to be established by the United States and Japan. It is unfortunate that Japan has to face monetary difficulties because of Tsunami tragedy and it will be some time before it would be able to provide financial aid to other countries. It would be strategically wise to include Australia to carry out this mission and goal. Australia is in this position to extend financial and other related assistance to South East Asian countries.

In due course of time, China would like to extend its influence and leadership role in East and South Asian countries. In spite of billion of dollars aid to

Pakistan from the United States, it considers China as the most valuable partner and not U.S.A. China has already established good relations with its neighbors and it would resent the influence of the United States. To counter this move, U.S.A, Japan and Australia have to play their desired role. It would not be a wrong assumption that India would challenge the Chinese incursions. China would team up with Russia and U.S would form a group with Japan, Australia and India in it. Global politics never stays still; new alignments would be formed. United States has to carve its foreign policy to cater to the needs of the regional countries.

One of the most up coming countries of East Asia is South Korea; it ranks amongst the top ten economies of the world. It would be in the interest of the United States to provide advanced military training, latest military hardware and substantial monetary aid to strengthen the South Korean army. United States has to have military personnel from Australia, South Korea and Japan to sustain its operations in full force, in this region. Political pundits hold the view that Russia and China together, would form a formidable group to lessen the global influence of the United States and its allies in the coming decades. However, Russia would not enter the Asian territory-it would be China that would like to dictate its terms to the Asian countries.

China wants to show to the world that its way of conducting business, military supremacy, political dictatorship and suppressing freedom of speech and other human rights work well and bring prosperity to the average citizen of the country. United States has the obligation to prove to the citizens of the world that it is not true. It has to chart out clear cut policies to assist developing countries to follow the path of true democracy and uphold the banner of freedom of speech, thought and action. Prosperity without these freedoms means nothing.

Why U.S and Japan needs each other

Let us look into similarities of these two countries. From an absolute monarchy to a robust democracy, Japan has changed a lot. It is highly westernized, technologically advanced and business savvy country. With a population of more than hundred millions, the Gross Domestic Product exceeds five trillions. It is the most reliable source of electronic goods and automobiles. The national per capita income is around forty thousand dollars. United States needs Japan as a trading partner; it also needs it for its surplus foreign reserve to be invested in the U.S treasury fund. In case of any unforeseen aggression or confrontation against China or Russia, United States needs a country like Japan to come to its help. Highly trained personnel and solid reliability are needed in such situations.

Japan needs the United States for its safety and peaceful existence. China and Japan were never cozy to each other. In the twenty first century, China would emerge as the most powerful nation of Pacific Asia. In the past, it was Japan which had posed danger to the Asian countries. Now, it would be China. It is already spreading its world power image in Indonesia, Burma, Sri Lanka and other countries. Japan has lost its position as a military power after World War II. To counter any aggression from China or any other country, Japan has to have the military backing of the United States.

The Japanese government pays for all the expenses incurred by the U.S military personnel, stationed in Japan, but it saves a bundle for not spending sizeable amount on military budget. That is taken care by Uncle Sam. This savings means a lot in terms of business investment for the country. Billions of dollars are invested in creating new businesses, establishing higher educational institutes for research and development, healthcare, social welfare and other national priorities. This protection umbrella has helped Japan, tremendously.

The good part in U.S-Japan partnership is the mutual exclusiveness of national interests. There are no serious contentions of disagreements on global issues. In fact, there exist many areas of common interests. Development of South East Asia is good for both countries; they should pool their resources to assist these countries and thus create prosperity and peace in that area.

United States should prop up the political influence of Japan by supporting it to become a member of the Security Council. It should also support the membership of Germany, India and Brazil. These three countries would, most probably, help United States in many areas of global politics. The foreign policy of the United States has to have the dynamism of quick and appropriate changes; the past allies may not be the best allies-new changing circumstances have to be taken into account. A glaring example of this is Pakistan. South Korea, Japan, Australia and India could form a solid group to keep an eye on the aggressiveness of Chinese moves. In the long run, China and Russia would like to lessen the influence of he United States in Asia and else where.

ADVERSARIES

Friends and foes change positions as time moves on. History never remains constant. It is very true with nations just as it is with individual human beings. Considering the present world situation, United States has potentially, three adversaries to account for. They are China, North Korea and Iran. The situation may change; North Korea has now a new head of the state-Kim Jong Un, the son of the old dictator Kim Jong II. In his New Year message, the President of South Korea Lee Myabgk has conveyed a friendly message to the North Korean government to start a new chapter between the two countries. North Korea needs financial assistance, food and all kinds of help to alleviate its grim situation that is prevailing in the country for decades. If the young North Korean leader decides to change the course of his country policies, it would auger well not only for North Korea but for the whole world. South Korea along with United States and other western countries can change the miserable lives of the average North Korean citizen if the North Korean government let go its so called nuclear program. A foe could become a friend, under these conditions.

The condition of Chinese adversarial movement would be dictated by many socio-economical and political global factors. China is advancing rapidly towards a Super-Power status and United States has to confront this situation willingly or with doubts. As a mature nation China will not embark on a confrontational situation without measuring all pros and cons. It seems probable that for few more decades, it will stay in the background and the world would be spared from any major conflict. However, the distant future would see more of Chinese influence not only in Asia but through out the world. Like the pre world war II Japan, China would march on to take a dominant position in the world affairs. Not only United States and other western powers, Russia too has to keep itself abreast of this upcoming scenario.

Iran is another country that could cause chaos in the world if it becomes a nuclear power. The present President of Iran Ahmadinejad is a revolutionary; he would not care for what happens to the world by his egoistical maniac actions. He would be the first person as he says to use nuclear weapons to demolish Israel. However, it might never happen. Israel might take the first step and finish off the race. NATO countries and United States are pushing the sanctions against Iran but would it work? It is a serious matter; no country would like to see a situation which resulted in Iraqi War. It is unfortunate that Iran has a dictatorial regime and the general public is powerless. Under these conditions, it would be a difficult task to change the nuclear plans of the Iranian government. Iranian public, on the other hand can change this situation. Western countries should openly court the Iranian citizens to accept western help and forget their nuclear ambitions. This strategy might work for the good of all nations.

In the mean time, United States has to be ready to face these three potentially dangerous nuclear powers. The present thinking of North Koreans and Iranian leaders lead us to believe that these nations would not abandon their nuclear programs unless some really radical events take place in their countries

CHINA

The history of China goes back to four thousand years. The most famous son of China is Kongfuzi, well known by the name of Confucius. He was born around 500 B.C. China had a long history of kings and queens till Sun Yat Sen disposed off the monarchy headed by a queen. General Chiang ki Shek succeeded Sun Yat Sen. He was the head of the Nationalist Kuomintang Party (KMT). At the same time, Mao Tse Tung was engaged in the civil war that was going on in China. KMT and Chinese Communist Party were fighting against the Japanese occupation. General Chiang Ki Shek was a friend of the United States. The United States was supporting the General against Mao Tse Tung. The civil war went on for two decades and finally Mao Tse Tung forces defeated the Nationalists KMT. Chiang Ki Shek and his army had to flee the mainland China and move to Taiwan. Mao declared his victory and established the Peoples Republic of China in 1949.

The first Industrial Revolution took place in England in the eighteen century; the second revolution occurred in China during 1979-2000. Thirty million people were moved out of the poverty level to prosperity; a feat of great accomplishment and pride. The Communist Government showed to the world what it could do just in three decades. Indeed, never in the history of the world so many people moved to higher standards of living in such a short period of time. Peoples Republic of China became a role model for others to follow especially the emerging countries of Asia and Africa.

Starting as an agricultural country, China now has taken number two position in the world economy .With 5.4 trillion Gross Domestic Product, it has overtaken Japan in 2011 but it is lagging far behind the United States economy of fifteen trillions. However, China's economy is moving at a zooming speed of ten to twelve percent per annum; with this rate, China could compete strongly with the United States in 2030. No other country, at this moment, is sitting at this pivotal position.

It is interesting to note that Chiang Ki Shek forces were defeated in mainland China, yet the diplomatic relations were still maintained with the Nationalist KMT and not with the Communist Government. Only in 1979, the United States recognized the Peoples Republic of China.

Mao wanted to transform China in a big hurry. He started Great Leap Forward Movement in 1958. This movement was to introduce collective farming and control all agricultural activities, in China; something very similar to Russian State Farming model. All the land was owned by the government and the crop was the government property. It is said that millions died of famine and starvation, as a result of this communist devised ideology. This traumatic failure did not stop Mao to start his new so called Cultural Revolution in 1966. Through the backdoor of this revolution, Mao wanted to purge all his opponents and destroy all forms of arts and culture from the Chinese society. Strict communist ideology and personal patriotic actions as interpreted by Mao were published in so called Red Books and were distributed throughout China, to be followed by all citizens. Like Stalin, Mao wanted to be treated like a God Father and like, Stalin he was instrumental in killing millions of his own people. It is irony of history that dictators kill thousand of people and still retain their picture in their national currency notes. It is no-doubt that Mao consolidated the country into one nation but at what price?

It was President Nixon who recognized the value of China Card. The Cold War between the United States and Russia was going strong; Nixon and his Secretary Of State, Dr.Kissinger thought that leveraging China against Russia would be a good policy. So in 1972, Nixon went to China and met with Mao. China was also looking forward to establishing good relations with the United States. It had invaded India in 1962 and had border disputes with Russia in 1969. China needed some support for its actions against India and Russia.

Mao died in 1976 and Deng Xiaoping became the top Chinese official. He took a u turn from Mao's policies and opened the door of prosperity for China. He went to Singapore and Japan and observed how these two countries transformed themselves into sizzling economies. He set up Special Economic Zones where the government provided tax incentives and other facilities to private businesses so that they can export goods to foreign countries at bargain prices. This Communist turned Capitalist was sold on Capitalism; he used to say: wealth is good for you. He visited the United States and established friendly working relations between the two countries. Mao had united the country but it was Deng who transformed China to become an economic giant.

China adopted Open door policy to foreign investors in 1986 and this action gave a big boost to industrialization in different sectors of the economy. Giant multinational corporations like General Motors, I.B.M, General Electric and many others invested heavily in Chinese manufacturing. With its low wage advantage and lax government regulations, China gradually moved to become the manufacturing workshop of the world. At this juncture, it is difficult to beat the Chinese made product in terms of price and reasonable quality. The Chinese government is keeping its currency low-undervalued-to gain huge advantage in terms of price. No wonder it has built a trillion dollar foreign reserve in its treasury deposits.

Though China was making economic progress by leaps and bounds with an annual growth rate over ten percent, yet the country was not making any headway in terms of personal freedom and related human rights. A cross section of the Chinese society thought that this is the time to rise against the Communist rule and go for a democratic way of life. Young students from college and universities along with others erected a replica of Statue of Liberty in the sprawling grounds of Tiananman Square and staged a peaceful demonstration against Beijing government; this event took place in 1989. For few days, the Communist government waited and asked the demonstrators to leave but when they did not, the tanks rolled in and fired on unarmed citizens. Thousands died for the sake of freedom and democracy. The whole world condemned the Chinese government but that was the beginning and the end of freedom movement in China. The United States and other western countries realized that it would not be easy to change the basic structure of a communist government.

U.S FOREIGN POLICIES TOWARDS CHINA

Global Supremacy: At this juncture of history, United States has the greatest influence on the world stage-economically and militarily. Let us check how China stands against the United States on military grounds. These are the statistics:

U.S.A	2010	CHINA
Military Budget: 729 billion		78 billion
Active Personnel: 1.58 million		2.26 million
Aircraft Carriers: 11		None
Stealth Fighters: 139		None
Submarines: 71		65
Nuclear Warheads: 9,400		240
Fighter Planes: 2379		1320

Recently-2011-one of the top Generals of China, Gen.Chen made a statement that China will not match the military power of the United States. On financial side, U.S.A has an economy of fifteen trillions versus China's 5.4 trillions. At this point, China's Gross Domestic Product is moving at ten percent or more. The Gross National Income of China is $ 4000 per capita; the GNI for U.S.A is around $48,000 or more.

China is miles apart from the United States; the chances are that it may not be able to catch up with the United States, at any time. It is true China will be moving aggressively in that direction, however, the United States has many pluses that will keep it far ahead of China for twenty to thirty years, minimum.

The foreign policies of the United States have to look from this scenario: what would happen if China and Russia –together-decide to launch a military attack on the United States or its allies in Europe or Asia. Are the Deterrent and Containment policies are in place, at this time? Are the policy makers of Washington thinking on these lines? Idiot dictators and arrogant political leaders can make decisions that could throw the world in holocaust. However, the chances for these scenarios are slim. It will start a global war which nobody wants it.

It is very apparent that China will start exercising its global stature in Asia and Africa as its economic and military position is strengthened. The United States can take a cooperative position or oppose Chinese moves. Realities might dictate the United States not to be present at every place. However where ever the interests of the United States are involved, it should not shy away from taking that responsibility with courage and prudence.

A very dangerous situation could arise if China along with Pakistan invades India. The Defense Minister of India, Mr. Antony made a statement, recently that we have to get ready for this situation. India is likely to go to the United

States for its help, in that scenario. The United States should be ready to respond to this call. Russia might remain neutral or side with China, in this clash. Judging Pakistan, at this junction, it could be predicted that it will be the breeding ground for terrorists and Islamic fundamentalists creating trouble for India, U.S.A, England and other western countries.

Human Rights: The leading most country in the world where human rights are trampled to dust is China. There are other countries like Burma-now called Maymar-where freedom of speech, freedom to oppose dictatorship and other human rights are crushed by the military junta. By all moral and ethical standards, these countries should be condemned by all freedom loving people.

All of us want happiness in our lives; no doubt, money is a big source for making people happy. But we have to ask: Is freedom more important than money? The answer is "Yes". The present Chinese leaders and the past Stalin supporters might disagree. The citizens of the civilized world, however, would give a big thumb up to doctrines of freedom.

Mao, like Hitler and Stalin was the symbol of oppression and death. Millions died under Mao's regime. The present Chinese leaders are not like Mao but they are miles away from the real meaning of democracy and freedom of thought. In 2010, Liu Xiaoboa, a Chinese dissident was awarded the Nobel Prize for Peace. He wanted to change the existing political set up of Labor Camps, Torture and suppression of human rights in China. The Chinese government put him in jail for eleven years and when the Nobel Prize was announced, his wife too, was put behind bars. This is the recent episode in the Chinese history of repression. Another notable chapter of uprising against the ruthless Chinese government was Tiananman Square, back in 1989. People can never forget the picture of a protester, unarmed, standing in front of a moving military tank. He was prepared to sacrifice his life for the sake of freedom.

The leaders of the Communist Chinese government tell the world that these kinds of freedom which the western countries hold sacred are not relevant in case of China. Strangely enough President Putin in his hey days criticized the concept of democracy as practiced in the western world as alien to the Russian way of thinking-a similar thought which the Chinese leaders are saying today. Russia and China have a long way to go to be called democratic and free.

What should be the policies of the United States towards China to redress the present condition of human rights? Shall it remain a silent spectator or speak out loud? We must not forget what President Reagan told the Russians: Tear down this wall, Mr.Gorbachev. We have to stand up against tyranny and injustice wherever it exists. The only way dictators are put to sleep, are bold and courageous moves. United States stands for some cherished noble principles of human behavior; its Constitution guarantees the freedom of speech, freedom to worship and freedom to act-as long as it is peaceful in nature. These are the pillars of western democratic structure and the world believes in it except few non believers.

The question that has to be answered is how much pressure should be exerted against the Chinese government for violating these human rights. Some observers suggest that in due course of time, the average Chinese person would have more freedom to speech and more freedom to reform as time moves on. It will be a wait and see scenario; nothing would be sure.

As the most powerful democracy in the world, it is the utmost responsibility of the United States to unfurl the flag of freedom to all the places of the world. People do not change. Countries do not change, unless they are forced to do so.

Best Business Practices: China has become the manufacturing workshop of the world. Apparels, Toys, Shoes and other daily use commodities that are used through out the globe, are now, made in China. It is very difficult to beat the Chinese prices because China enjoys a very big advantage of low wages and subsidized government duties and taxes. It is repeating the Japanese phenomenon which took place decades ago.

Most of the items produced in China are made for export. There are very few countries in the world which have a positive trade balance with China. In most cases, it is China which has a big surplus. Last year-2010-United States had a negative trade balance of $270 billions. Many countries including European Union had lodged protest to China for its dumping practices in Europe and Asia. Jack Welsh, the ex G.E Chief had said: Chinese are sharp business people; beware!

The strategy that Chinese government is adopting is to keep its currency, Yuan low compared to dollar and Euro. That makes its products cheaper in the world market. The United States has held many meetings with the Chinese government to raise the Yuan exchange rate against the dollar but so far nothing tangible has happened. The Chinese officials are not budging from their position. They know this is how China has amassed trillions of dollars in foreign exchange. The Chinese government knows that it has nothing to lose if Yuan remains low. It is up to the governments of the United States and other countries to firm up their positions and deliver a kind of ultimatum to the Chinese that if they do not change their policy than other countries would be free to impose additional tariff duties on the Chinese goods. It would be considered a fair business practice under those conditions. The global trade prospers when every country plays its part on equitable basis. China would have to comply with the best business practices, sooner or later.

China became a member of World Trade Organization in 2001; United States supported its membership. Each member of this organization has to observe its rules and regulations; the Chinese government on the other hand has set up its own procedures that favor the Chinese companies. At the Annual Strategic and Economic Dialogue between U.S.A and China, held in Washington in 2011, Treasury Secretary Timothy Geithner and Commerce Secretary Gary Locke raised the questions of low exchange rate of Yuan and discrimination against American and other foreign companies, operating in China. As usual, the Chinese officials denied the charges. At the same time, the Chinese expressed concerns about the U.S annual deficit which has crossed 1.4 trillions. China is the biggest lender to the United States, at this juncture. If the value of the dollar goes down in the financial markets, China would suffer a big loss-they want some kind of assurance. It seems that China would gradually let Yuan go up in exchange, against foreign currencies; presently it is undervalued by 15-40%.

Foreign policies directed towards China whether they are related to Human Rights, Global and Regional Area of Influence or Financial and Business Matters, would be difficult to enforce on an authoritarian Communist regime. Sharp diplomatic tools would be needed similar to those which were used while dealing with the Russians after World War II.

Second Cold War: When the World War II ended in 1945, a new war started and that was Cold War. Russia, United States and other western allies, were enmeshed in this War of Words. Spying and counter spying operations were in full swing. The leaders of these two polarizing groups were ready to fight out every nickel and dime issues. Diplomats were expelled out, off and on but the real guns were still not smoking. This scenario lasted for almost forty years till 1991 when the great U.S.S.R disintegrated into a shadow of its past. The honors for ending this war of words should be given to Reagan and Gorbachev who put an end to this potentially explosive situation and created an environment of mutual trust and respect.

Luckily, the first decade of the twenty first century went by without making too much noise. The Russian President Putin did start a mini cold war with the United States over the nuclear defense shield to be set up in Poland. President Bush was pushing for this plan but Obama dropped it and the Russians were happy. It looks like that it would be China that would be raising its voice against the United States or Japan over issues like Taiwan, sovereignty of few small islands off China Sea or Darfur. It should be noted that China has not yet reached that point of inflection that Russia had when it was raising all kind of hell. There should not be any doubt, that very soon China too, would start behaving in a similar fashion. It would begin when it would feel confident about its clout in the global political stage.

United States would come directly into picture when there would be any question over Taiwan or shipping lanes over the sea in Pacific and South East Asia. Down the road, China may not like the presence of American fleet in that region. What would happen then? The Cold War would swing into action. U.S.A, Japan, India and China could start a war in that region if for some reason there is no meeting ground between them.

If we sort out areas of agreement and disagreements between China and the United States, we can come to some fair conclusions. It could be said with solid reasoning that China and the United States would never go for a direct hit against each other over Taiwan. China would never dare to challenge the United States. The permanent solution of the Taiwan problem is the maintenance of the status quo; let the present fluid condition be kept for good-no change. It will keep the peace for that region Taiwan and China could co exist without creating any problem. China does want good relations with Iran and North Korea. United States has labeled these two countries as Evil. China opposed the sanctions that the western countries wanted to impose upon Iran. In the background the United States want the Chinese help to resolve the problems with North Korea. China can utilize its friendship with North Korean leaders and erase out one big factor of cold war rhetoric China and the United States have genuine case of mutual interest over exchange rate of Yuan, Human Rights and international shipping lanes in Asia. Both sides have to observe the guided principles of business. would have no significance of any dimension.

IRAN

Let us recapture some of the important links between Iran and the United States. Iran also known as Persia was one of the staunchest friends of the United States. Back in 1972, President Nixon praised the Shah of Iran in glorious terms and promised the United States assistance in setting up nuclear reactors in Iran to generate electricity. The Shah and his queen were the most welcomed guests in the White House. President Carter, while on a visit to Tehran in 1976, said that the Shah is the stabilizing force in the Middle East. Those were the days of cordial and robust friendship between Iran and the United States.

Things changed when the Shah was overthrown in 1979 in a revolution staged and supported by the Iranian religious clerics headed by Ayatollaha Khomeni. The history of Iran nosedived by fifty years. The Shah had become an autocratic ruler and lost the touch with his people. The Shah and his cronies, the elite group and the military were running the country without paying any attention to the common man on the street. The result was rampant corruption, unemployment and wide spread dissatisfaction with the regime.

It has been said again and again that the United States has supported kings and dictators who did not pay any attention to the welfare of the common man and woman of their country. Those policies were wrong and should have been addressed to set up democratic structure in those countries rather than supporting autocratic rulers.

1979 saw a turning point in the relations of the United States and Iran. This was the year when Khomeni returned from France and became the ruler of Iran. The exiled Shah was diagnosed with Cancer and he wanted to get medical treatment in the United States. When the Shah was granted the humanitarian request, radical anti American Iranians went bizarre. Many professors, administrators and students from the American University in Tehran were taken hostage and were brutally tortured by the religious Iranian fanatics. These American citizens had to suffer terribly-mentally and physically-the inhumane treatment for almost a year before they were freed at the beginning of Reagan presidency in 1980.

The days of dictators and autocratic rulers are disappearing fast in our changing world. The Iranian people threw away the despotic regime of the Shah and at the same time embraced the religious Shariahs laws set up by Ayatollas. The country was turned upside down; nothing moved without the approval of Mullahas of Islamic Republic. Anti-American fervor became the popular flavor of the Iranian society. United States became the most hated country in the eyes of the general public of Iran. Muslim clerics reigned over all socio-economic activities. The western culture was shunned and disapproved by the masses as a symbol of decay and blasphemy.

It is recognized universally that Revolutions bring new ideas, vibrant actions and colossus changes in the society. Let us watch what happens in Iran now.

New Geo-political Structure

After the fall of the Shah and the rise of Ayatollas, the governing structure of the country stood on four pillars of power, namely (a) Influential Muslim Clerics (b) Hard line Conservatives (c) Moderates (d) Pro-West minority.

Religion plays an important role among people when they are unemployed, lack means of support, not educated and see no future for them and their families. A big cross section of the Iranian general public was undergoing through stress and strains of the daily living while the Shah and his selected group of people were having good times. Ayatolla Khomeni provided a way out of this misery and by the will and approval of the Iranian people he became their de facto ruler. Religion took over all the activities of the government and the Muslim clerics started dictating the socio-economic life of the country. All the major decisions of the government have to have the approval of these Ayatollas.

The political scene was dominated by the Hard line Conservatives who had the support of the Muslim Clerics and religious fanatics. These hard liners are anti-America and think that the American government is plotting to overthrow the present Ayatoolas regime. This group of people considers Israel as their enemy number one; they want to develop nuclear weapons and vow to establish Muslim supremacy. The present President of Iran, Mr.Ahmadinejad is the spoke person of this political section. He is giving hard time to western countries regarding nuclear plants operations especially to enrichment of Uranium.

The Moderate leaders are not entirely opposed to the United States and want to maintain normal relations with the west. They feel that financial assistance and other kind of help from the United States, in education, health and military build up would be good for Iran. This section wants to retain the basic tenants of the western culture. They do not want to follow the Ayatollas blindly. These people want to keep the movement of the modern days thinking in their daily life. Young and educated Iranians belong to this group.

Pro-west minority group represents mainly business class. They do not like the ruling Ayatollas to hold on to power. They want to be part of the mainstream of the world present day movements, economically, socially and politically. Their interest is not hundred percent pro nuclear; they want progress in the country in all the fields. Last year-2010-huge protests were staged by the Pro West and Moderates against the Mullahas and Ahmadinejad regime. The protest resulted in many deaths and did not succeed in its objectives.

What policies of the United States should be, towards these four political parties –that question has to be addressed. At this juncture, the hard liners are in the majority. Most of the Iranians are anti-America, anti-Israel and pro-Palestine. When President Bush named Iran as an Evil Empire, it did not go well with the Iranian citizens. It made them angry and determined to wage war against the western countries. A hard line approach may be difficult to impose on the Iranian government and the results might not be successful. In this context, the sanctions that the western countries along with the United States are thinking to apply against the Iranian government may not work. Iran has good natural assets of oil and gas. Only very drastic measures of embargo on shipment of oil might work; over all it would be very difficult to achieve results.

Nuclear Realities

Why does the Iranian President keep on telling the world that our nuclear program is only for peaceful purpose? The answer to this question is: he is trying to buy as much time as he can get. According to International Atomic Energy Agency (IAEA) information, Iran is not far behind in successfully carrying out its nuclear tests-may be few years. President Ahmadinejad feels that if India and Pakistan could defy the world by testing their nuclear weapons, in 1998, then Iran should go ahead and do the same. But the big difference in the Iranian case is that Israel would not consider it safe to see the nuclear weapons in the hands of its arch enemy which vows to wipe out its existence. It is a very dangerous situation. If Iran reaches that stage and Israel decides to attack and demolish the plant sites, the whole Muslim world would rise against the United States, Israel and western countries. There are no if and but questions on this issue-it is a surety. It would not only be the Pakistan, Afghanistan and Chehnya's suicide bombers, Al Qaeda and Taliban militants that would turn against the non Muslim world but it would be the whole Muslim population that would revolt against the west. This might turn out to be very explosive situation.

Pakistan is the only Muslim country which possesses nuclear weapons. Many political pundits have said that Iranian leadership wants to dominate the Muslim world which could be accomplished by having nuclear weapons. It may be pointed out that Iran is a Shiite Muslim state; the majority of the Muslim population in the world however, is Sunni. Shiite and Sunnis are not friendly to each other. Saudi Arabia, a Sunni Muslim State is the richest among the Muslim countries. It does not want Iran to take over the leadership of the Muslim world. It should be understood very clearly that all Muslim countries are in favor of an independent Palestine State and the degree of animosity towards Israel differs from state to state. Taking into consideration these factors, the United States has to formulate its policy towards Iran in such a way that it keeps the Muslim world on its side and at the same time persuade Iran to give up its nuclear ambition. It will not be easy; most of the Iranians are in favor of becoming a nuclear power so that they could stand against Israel on an equal footing.

Iran has large reserves of oil and gas; it does not have to have nuclear reactors to generate electricity for its industry and homes. When President Ahmadinejad says that we are interested in developing nuclear energy just for peaceful purposes, it looks like he is not telling the truth; there is something more than that. If the western countries offer to Iran attractive package of incentives for not going nuclear, it may give up its plans. Political pressure from Russia and China may play some role in this scenario. Iran has been dodging the efforts of the IAEA to let the world know where Iran stands at this point in its quest to become nuclear. Off and on, some statements are released by the Iranian government that they are very close to enrichment process of Uranium. It is but sure that Iranians would continue their efforts and at the same time deny that they are ready to explode their nuclear bombs.

If the United States and other western countries play some internal politics and bend the thinking of the Moderates and Pro-west minority in favor of attractive incentives for Iran, it would be a great diplomatic victory.

While laying down strategic policies towards Iran, the following key points should be kept in view. They are:

Sanctions against Iran would not deliver the desired results; it would consolidate the Hard line Conservatives who hate the United States and England. Calling Iran as Evil Empire was a mistake.

The general public of Iran would not accept any proposals put up by the United States or England

Russia and Germany are the two countries who can exert some influence on the Iranian government. Iran had kept good relations with Russia, in the past and it is a major supplier of military hardware to Iran. Germany is the largest economy of Europe and it can provide attractive financial assistance to Iran.

The problem of Palestine is the biggest hurdle in solving the Middle East Crisis. Relations between Israel and other Muslim countries revolve around Palestine. Support of the United States to Israel, has made the Muslim world anti-United States.

Stick and carrot policy might work with Iran. The efforts of the western countries should be to prolong the time frame of enriching the Uranium to nuclear grade, by offering different options to Iran.

Strict compliance of non transferable nuclear technology to Iran from other countries should be enforced. In the past Pakistan had been involved in sharing nuclear technology with Iran, North Korea and perhaps Libya.

If the Iranian government is stalled in its nuclear technology, the people of Iran might start looking seriously to other options; they might like to have attractive financial incentives to create more jobs and better health and education programs for their country.

As long as the Palestine problem remains open, Iranian nuclear program would remain in the forefront. Israel has to look into the seriousness of this situation and should make some tangible concessions to the Arab demands. In place of one hostile front, it will be facing two deadly enemies-Iran and Palestine. Creating an environment for free Independent Palestine State, the whole world would be spared from a catastrophic annihilation. The policies of the United States have to have some inviting fresh ideas to woo the Palestinians; meeting not all the demands of the Israeli government may be a better solution. After all, pluses and minuses of the alternative conditions are jittery and explosive situations; they are not good for Israel, Palestine, United States or the rest of the world. This is an important consideration for all the concerned parties to examine, with its full impact on the whole world.

The influence of the Muslim clerics governing body might start losing its hold on the general public of Iran, as time goes by. The hard line Conservatives will not be able to convince the Iranian citizens to keep on spending resources on developing nuclear weapons if no tangible result shows up in the near future. Moderates and Pro west groups would then have good chances of propagating their views and winning more people to their side. Western countries should watch those signs and take their move. The United States policies have to have solid support of the European nations because Iran has more confidence in dealing with the Europeans than with the United States.

Three Pronged Strategies:

Iranian nuclear program has taken the worlds attention; United States and other western countries are threatening Iran to comply with the United Nation resolutions or face tough sanctions. IAEA keeps on issuing present status of Iranian nuclear program on a regular interval; however, nothing tangible has come out of it. President Ahmadinejad has stood firm and does not budge from his position.

To solve this tricky problem, we are proposing three proposals.

(a) Offer a non-aggression peace treaty

(b) Establish a good Assistance Package

(c) Enforce a strict examination program

Non-Aggression Peace Treaty: Most of the Iranians believe that United States want to overthrow the Ayatollas regime and replace it with Pro-West government. If this notion be erased by offering a Peace Treaty to Iran, it would help a lot in removing many apprehensions and doubts about United States intentions. The feelings of hostility and animosity towards United States would diminish drastically. And hopefully this would start a new chapter in the U.S – Iranian relations.

Good Assistance Package: If U.S and other western countries come up with an attractive assistance program to Iran, there are good chances that the Iranian government may just forget about its nuclear plan and accept this generous aid package. After all, Iran does need aid in the areas of higher education, health plans and technology. Non Aggression Pact along with Assistance Program would be welcomed by the general public of Iran.

Strict Examination Program: The United Nation through IAEA should convey to Iranian government that it will have no problem with its peaceful nuclear program provided IAEA is totally in charge of overseeing its all activities. If Iran is engaged only in peaceful nuclear operations, it would be alright. In such a situation, there would not be any sanctions against the Iranian government and it can go ahead with its plans.

As pointed out before, Sanctions against Iran would not have any positive outcome; it will only reinforce the influence of the Hard line Conservatives and religious radicals and fanatics. The general public of Iran wants to see better living conditions, better opportunities and brighter future for future generations. Nuclear weapons do not generate any of those above mentioned conditions. It is good for dictators and ego maniacs to keep on boasting on having nuclear bombs. This is very true for North Korea and Iran. Both of these countries are governed by dictators and autocrats.

It is our opinion that any of the three strategies-individually or combination of two or all of them combined-would be very helpful in resolving this explosive situation. Palestine and Israeli conflict would have to be resolved at the same time. The foreign policy of the United States towards Iran has to be drawn, based upon these important points of views. It is in the interest of the United States to make friendship with as many Muslim countries as possible, for its own safety and welfare. It might take a few decades for Iran to become a close friend of the United States but it is worth trying.

NORTH KOREA

When the World War II ended in 1945, Russians in the north and Americans in the south occupied the Korean peninsula; the dividing line of control was at 38th parallel. In 1948, Russians moved out and Russian trained Kim Il Sung declared Peoples Republic of Korea an independent state. The American occupied Korea declared its independence in 1950 and that started the invasion from the north. The Korean War lasted till 1953; no peace treaty was signed but 38th parallel became the de facto line of demarcation between North and South Korea.

Just like East and West Germany, North Korea followed the Communist platform of the government and South Korea embraced the Capitalistic model of government. Like East Germany, North Korea with a population of about twenty four million people was ruled by a Communist dictator Kim Sung. By all standards, it was a totalitarian and ruthless form of government. It was reported that there were about 200,000 political prisoners; there were forced abortions, public executions and complete suppression of individual rights.

Russian Communism was thriving in sixties and North Korea was a big benefactor of the Russian aid. The country made good progress in terms of industrialization. In 1972 North and South Korea held talks for unification of the country. When the Russian empire crumbled in 1991, it made a devastating impact on other Communist countries including North Korea. All the aid packages were folded up. The rulers of North Korea had decided to embrace nuclear program. At the same time, it allowed the inspection of their nuclear operations to the representatives of International Atomic Energy Agency. That was year 1992 and two years later when North Korean Dictator Kim Sung died, North Korea announced that it has frozen its nuclear program. One year later, the United States agreed to build two nuclear reactors for commercial use along with financial assistance to the government of North Korea. Things were looking good at that point in time in terms of U.S-North Korean relations.

Kim Jong Il succeeded his father and became the President of North Korea. He followed his father's doctrines and policies to govern the country with an iron hand. In 1996, North Korea faced natural calamities of flood and famine. About two million people died due to starvation and other causes. Faced with harsh realities of shortage of oil, fertilizer and food, the government leaders thought of making nuclear program as a leverage to get attention from the United States; to secure security and massive financial assistance. This leveraging policy became the focal point of North Korean government bargaining chip towards South Korea, the United States and the western countries.

Year 2000, saw a new chapter in the relations between North and South Korea. President of South Korea Kim Dae-jung made a trip to Pyonyang, the capital city of North Korea and announced a policy of friendship and fraternity; it was named Sunshine Policy. This gesture was made to help the North Korean people who were facing starvation, ill health, unemployment and all kinds of other problems. Thousand of North Koreans were escaping to China and South Korea because of the harsh realities of daily life. The common citizen was not in a position to revolt against the powerful dictatorship.

The North Korean government made zigzag movements towards the United States. All along, the Korean leadership was trying to get as much financial aid as well as food, oil and other essential needs, as possible. And at the same time, it was announcing to the world that it is developing nuclear weapons for its security. Almost every year, the government would change its policy; sometime it wanted reconciliation with the United States and at other occasion it would abort its promises and start threatening South Korea and the United States. During the year 2000, North Korea sent a high profile delegation to the United States to establish good working relations. President Clinton sent his Secretary of State Madame Albright to North Korea to reinforce this peace initiative. Unfortunately, this move failed to materialize when President Bush declared North Korea as Axis of Evil, in 2002; all the built up links of co operation and accommodation evaporated since then.

In 2002, North Korea announced that it has been working secretly on nuclear program and it has reactivated its Yongbyon nuclear reactor. Furthermore, the observers from International Atomic Energy Agency were barred by the North Korean government. Next year, the government said that it has enough Plutonium to make nuclear weapons. Defying the United Nations and the United States, North Korea made a bold announcement in 2006 that it has successfully tested the nuclear device and would start making nuclear weapons for its safety against the possible attack from the United States and South Korea. President Bush's remarks against the North Korean dictatorship made collaboration in any form or shape, very difficult. The group of six countries namely Japan, China, Russia, South Korea, United States and England were thrown into back alley by North Korea. Once again a jittery feeling prevailed.

President elect Lee Myung bak reversed the Sun Shine Policy in 2008. He took a tough stand against the North Korean human rights violations and dictatorial rules and regulations. He stopped family reunions-between north and south-and withdrew aid program to North Korea. He was ready to provide assistance to the North Korea provided it abandons its nuclear program and restore normal democratic structure in the country. Left with no choice, the United Nations imposed sanctions against North Korea after it walked out of International talks, in 2009. North Korea did not care for Sanctions against the country and went on rampage by sinking one of the warships of South Korea in 2010. Serious border clashes occurred between the two countries. United States and South Korea in return staged a joint military exercise to show to the North Korean government their resolve and determination to meet the force with greater force and power. To escalate the matter further, North Korea declared that it is going to test its latest long range nuclear missiles which could reach the United States. Naturally, United States and other countries got alarmed with this announcement. Later on, it was found out that those missiles failed in their tests and proved to be "thuds". It provided a sense of relief to the United Nations, United States and South Korea. However, it showed that North Korea is determined to become a nuclear power whatever it may take. It has been reported that it already has one or two nuclear bombs but there are some doubts too, to this claim. Evil or not, North Korea is a dangerous country.

Options for United States

While charting out its policies towards North Korea, United States has to examine all facets of regional and global ramifications of its actions; where does North Korea stands today and what changes it has incorporated recently in its national structure-that have to be looked into.

Right now, North Korea is facing:
- (a) Desperate economic conditions
- (b) Negligible foreign investment
- (c) Shortage of oil, fertilizer and food
- (d) Starvation, Deplorable health conditions

The changes that have been made by the North Korean government to improve its economical conditions are:
- (a) Expanded foreign trade links
- (b) Introduced modern technologies in industries
- (c) Efforts are being made to attract foreign investments
- (d) Market oriented reforms are introduced to boost production.

It gives a clear idea that North Korea does want to stand on its own feet; however, it might take sometime to get to that stage.

Reacting to different posturing of the North Korean government, the United States has taken extreme stands of bombing the Yongbyon nuclear plant during President Clinton presidency back in 1994 to multi national peace proposal of South Korea, China and Japan (Sun Shine Policy)in 2000.

It is well said that if you corner an enemy, it will do any thing to defend itself; it is a true analogy in case of North Korea, at present. If the North Korean regime thinks that the United States is going to attack its nuclear plants, it might send its forces to attack South Korea. It has one of the largest standing army in the world-more than a million people in uniform. Seoul is just twenty five miles from demilitarized zone; one third of South Korean population lives near Seoul. A determined attack on South Korea could bring huge devastation to the country. It is true that there are about 38,000 American military personnel in South Korea and ultimately, North Korea would face serious consequences of its actions, yet it would be too late-damage would have been done already. It is imperative not to provoke North Korea but at the same time United States and the United Nations should not appease to its threats.

President Bush's tough policy of isolating North Korea and President Obama's approval of Sanctions against the country do not convey an approach of reconciliation and positive engagement. Instead of counter threats from the United States and South Korea, a middle of the road policy would be helpful in resolving the crisis with the North Korean government.

We must not forget that dictators move with their egos and false pride; they do not exercise rational judgment and they do not care for the ordinary citizen. It is therefore very important to be flexible and farsighted when dealing with such personalities. China, Japan and Russia have had long standing relations with the Korean leadership, in the past and they can play very useful role in convincing the North Korean leaders to abandon their nuclear program and accept badly needed assistance package from the United States and South Korea.

Can U.S stop North Korean Nuclear Program

The most critical question that has to be addressed: Is the United States in a position to stop North Korea to proceed with its Nuclear Program unilaterally or with the support of other countries like Russia, China and Japan? Analyzing the past record of North Korean government's declared policies it seems unlikely that North Korea would abandon its nuclear plan. North Korea and Iran, both are playing a waiting game. They will keep the western countries guessing and assuring sometime, that they are serious in abandoning their nuclear programs provided they (U.S and U.N) give them guarantee of financial assistance as well as food, oil, education, health and structural support.

The assumptions that the ordinary citizen would rise against the established dictatorship or the entrenched leadership would disintegrate do not stand a chance. The citizens of both countries have no power and have no support from any outside source. At the same time the dictatorial rule in North Korea and Iran are well entrenched. It would be rather an impossible task to replace or dismantle them.

North Korea and Iran are trying desperately to upgrade their know how of upgrading enriched Uranium to nuclear grade Plutonium and then assembling nuclear weapons, secretly-may be ten or twenty-before announcing to the world that they have become nuclear powers. At that stage they might even carry out successful nuclear tests to show to the world that they are not kidding and they have the nuclear weapons in their possession. Till that moment, they would continue to take zigzag positions of abandonment and possession of nuclear weapons of mass destruction- missiles and bombs.

There are countries like Russia and Pakistan that might supply the needed information to Iran; China, Pakistan and Russia may come to the help of North Korea. Pakistan's nuclear scientist Dr.Kadir had admitted that Pakistan has supplied nuclear technology to Iran, North Korea and Libya. Since every body knows about this, Russia, China and Pakistan may refrain from such activities. That would imply that local nuclear scientists would be the only source for North Korea and Iran to become full fledged nuclear nations. It may take two years or may take five; we can not predict. However, this is the time frame that International Atomic Energy Agency anticipates to take place.

Sanctions from the United States and the United Nations would not stop the North Korean leadership to abandon its nuclear program. Even Sun Shine policy of South Korea or providing food, oil and fertilizers would not make any dent in the program. Nuclear program has become a source of prestige and pride for the North Korean leaders. The money that could be utilized for other causes would be devoured by the military for carrying out its nuclear goals and targets. Dictators hardly care if thousand of people die of starvation or ill health. When Pakistan was developing its nuclear program, the Prime Minister of Pakistan at that time, Mr. Nawaz Sharif had said: we might have to eat grass but still we shall pursue our nuclear plan. This analogy holds correct in case of North Korea and Iran at this juncture. North Korean leaders want to show to the world that we are second to none. Iran, on the other hand wants to relay the message that we can destroy Israel. Under these conditions, serious planning has to be done.

Engagement versus Containment Policies

United States and other influential countries of the United Nations have to adopt Containment Policies along with Engagement and Cooperation with North Korean government. The best course of action would be to stretch the time frame for North Korea to become a nuclear power. As stated before, North Korea would not abandon its nuclear program since it is almost there. It would be in the interest of the United States and South Korea to keep talking with the North and provide assistance in terms of food, oil, education and health program. The purpose behind this is to save thousand of starving people and thus generating goodwill among the general public. The North Korean leadership would also appreciate this gesture from the United States and other countries like South Korea, China and Japan. In return, the North Korean government may freeze its nuclear program for a short period of time-just to take a breather-and allow IAEA staff to inspect its nuclear plants. However, after this short break, it is going to go full blast for its nuclear targets. It should not be a surprise to the United States. Containment policies like Sanctions against the flow of nuclear technology, procurement of nuclear hardware, trading in nuclear weapons as a supplier and other related areas should be enforced as a reminder that North Korea is not free whatever it wants to do related to the production of nuclear weapons. There would be restrictions and North Korea has to abide by the rules and regulations of the United Nations inspection process.

The world can not take any chances for an open confrontation with North Korea. South Korea would suffer the most if such a conflict occurs. Taking military action against the North by attacking nuclear plants could become a nightmare; China and Russia might turn against the West in such a situation. Simulating future projections in this scenario are not easy to predict. Unilateral action from the west could be a disaster; multilateral-United Nations-action may be difficult to achieve.

Two important factors namely solid cooperation and substantial financial aid to North Korea and secondly inability of North Korean Scientists to launch the nuclear program successfully within a short span of time, could trigger another direction for North Korea. The new leaders of North Korea may just write off the ambitious trajectory of becoming a full fledged nuclear power and in its place follow the flourishing and shining example of South Korea. In order to achieve this goal, important changes in policy settings have to be incorporated as soon as possible.

Taking hard line policies towards North Korea would not solve any problem- it would only aggravate the situation. It does not mean to let North Korea a free hand; strict controls have to be place and in addition an environment of mutual trust and friendship has to be created

Sometime, history of countries change with the change of Leadership; there was a chance in North Korea when Kim Jong IL passed away in December 2011 and his third son Kim Jong Un succeeded him as the new North Korean Commander in chief. Kim Jong Un is only in his mid twenties but he was immediately promoted as a four star general. It has been reported that it is his uncle who is running the show while he is under training.

Looking from the past history of North Korea, it seems that this young man may not be able to bring something fresh and new in terms of better relations with South Korea and the western countries. He is inexperienced and does not hold the power. Just after few months of his succession, Kim Jong Un announced the suspension of North Korean Nuclear Program in lieu of American Food Aid package. That was a good beginning; it was hoped that Kim Jong Un may depart from his dad's anti-west policies. However, it did not happen. It is too early to predict what this new head of the state is going to do in terms of Nuclear Program and establishing better and friendly relations with South Korea and the United States.

It is not only the United States that does not want to see North Korea as a nuclear power but it is China and most probably Russia, too that do not want to have their neighbor acquiring nuclear weapons. They are also skeptical about the leadership of the North Korean army generals. South Korea is the first country to be affected by the North Korean nuclear capabilities which in turn would affect the United States strategies. Presently the situation is calm and nothing new is happening. The international political scene is filled with Middle East situation and no new talks are being planned between North Korea and the western countries.

As mentioned before, the chances of putting a complete halt to the nuclear program are dim. North Korea like Iran is not going to abandon its nuclear dreams. Both of these countries have made this issue as a matter of national prestige and power politics. Inspite of the fact that North Korea is undergoing severe shortage of food and other necessities of life, the army and their politicians would not give up their arrogant attitude. It is unfortunate but these things are common in communist controlled countries even today.

When North Korea is going down the hill and South Korea is making strong progress in terms of national health and over all prosperity, the question of unification of North and South is out of the court yard. In a way it might be good for the United States too.

NON-ALIGNED

India and Indonesia were the two most prominent countries of Non Alignment Movement back in fifties. This group is still active and has a membership of almost fifty Asian and African countries. Non Alignment as it stands today means national interest; it has nothing to do with Russian or United States policies. After the collapse of Russian influence in 1991, India started moving towards the United States and began drifting away from Russia. Indian government headed by Dr. Man Mohan is pro America but it is not anti-Russian. In other words, India is neutral and non-aligned. Indian military force is equipped with Russian armaments –up to seventy percent but it does not have a military treaty with Russia or with the United States. Though India and China are logical adversaries, yet both of them profess their friendship for the other.

It is a matter of time, when China would be challenging American supremacy in the global policy making and India would have to decide what kind of relationship it would like to have with China, at that point in time. It would be a gradual process but China would definitely start exercising its economical and military muscle in that part of Asia, for sure, sooner than later. United States wants India to stand up and start leading in Asia but the Indian leadership is not ready for it as of now. China is building its military might and economical prosperity in a big manner and India is still struggling. Corruption, delays and incompetency in governance in India would make the country go slow and even stop the momentum which it had generated in the recent past. The Chinese government is highly motivated and autocratic but it is good for the national progress. United States has a big stake in present India and its future plans. To counter balance Chinese influence in Asia, United States has to take the help of India. Foreign policy of the United States must not forget this important agenda.

Indonesia is the largest Muslim population country, about two hundred forty million strong. It is a moderate Muslim country unlike Pakistan where orthodox Muslim culture is still thriving well. The present President of Indonesia, Susilo Yudhoyono is more pro than anti United States. It is interesting to note that President Obama had spent his childhood days in Indonesia when his mother was living in Jakarta. He wants to build good and strong relations with Indonesia. It must be noted that as an emerging developing country, Indonesia needs lot of help of every kind to make it move faster towards progress and national prosperity. United States is providing assistance in the area of Education, Health care and Agriculture, at the present moment but it should be maintained and increased in terms of money and duration. Just like India, Indonesia follows its own independent policy in foreign policy matters and does not follow either Russian or American coat tails.

Thailand has supported United States policies and had maintained good friendly relations with the United States. During the time when Thakin Shinawatra was Prime-Minister of Thailand, it appeared that the country is trying to lean towards Communist China. Thakin has been ousted, but his younger sister Yingluck Shnawatra has now become the new Prime-Minister Thailand is a valuable partner for the United States and it should be recognized.

INDIA

Some political observers have recorded that Franklin D.Roosevelt had talked to Winston Churchill, the British Prime-Minister to grant freedom to British India, after World War II. India became independent in 1947; Nehru became the Prime Minister of India. During the time when Nehru was studying at Oxford, Socialism was very much popular in British political circle. Nehru opted for a Socialist form of government for India-not capitalist or communist. He also wanted India not to side with the United States or with the United Soviet Socialist Republic-USSR. This policy created Non-Aligned Group of countries. India, China, Indonesia, Egypt, Yugoslavia became the co-founders of this federation. It gives a little background of India.

John F.Kennedy became the President of the United States in 1960. He wanted to establish close relations with India. He selected his own Harvard University Economic Professor John Galbraith as the ambassador to India. Somehow, Nehru and Professor Galbraith established good personal relations. The most glamorous and popular figure of that era, Mrs.Kennedy, the wife of the President, paid a state visit to India in 1961. Nehru welcomed her with enthusiasm. In 1962, China invaded India. The Indian army was no match to the Chinese assault. Nehru approached Kennedy and military supplies were immediately rushed to India. It was an important event in the U.S-India relations. At that particular juncture, Russia was the close ally of India.

Years rolled by; nothing spectacular happened between the United States and Indian relations till 1971 when India had dispatched military units to East Pakistan to support the Bangladesh independence movement. Pakistan forces suffered a most humiliating defeat and East Pakistan disappeared from the map. Mrs Indira Gandhi was the Prime Minister of India and Nixon was the President of the United States at that time. He and Dr.Henry Kissinger were outraged at the action of India. In the conversation with Henry Kissinger, Nixon called Mrs. Gandhi as "that bitch". This tells the kind of relations that were in place during Nixon presidency.

Carter succeeded Nixon; the U.S- India relations did change somewhat but not substantially. The real dramatic shift came when Bill Clinton became the U.S President. Like Kennedy, Bill realized the importance of good relations with India. By this time, there were about one million Indians that were living in the United States and they were one of the most successful communities of the country. Bill Clinton visited India and Atul Behari Bajpai, the Indian Prime-Minister paid a visit to the United States. Mr.Bajpai's party-Bhartiya Janta-was in favor of establishing close relations with the United States. During President Clinton's presidency the United States economy was doing pretty good; he increased the number of working visas-H1Visas- for Indians-that made Indians happy. Bill Clinton was popular with the Indian community. More Indians voted for Democratic candidates than to Republicans.

The turning point in U.S-India relations took place when George Bush became the U.S President. George Bush father-President George Bush Senior-was the American Ambassador to China, at one time; so China was not unfamiliar to George Bush Junior because he had lived there for sometime. President Bush was weighing the rising influence of China and the after effects of this new situation. The foreign policy of the United States had to address seriously the future ramifications of a rising China. China had fought war against the United States in Korea in 1950; it had border disputes with India and Russia. It was looking apparent that China, in the near future would pose a threat to the interests of the United States in the Asian sub-continent. To counter balance this potential threat, U.S.A had to look towards India as a matching partner to offset this possible dangerous scenario.

In 2005, Indian Prime-Minister, Dr.Singh paid a visit to the United States. During this visit, President Bush presented a highly controversial nuclear deal to Dr.Singh. Back in 1998, India had conducted nuclear tests, successfully; that had prompted President Clinton to impose sanctions against India. President Bush went out of his way to nullify these sanctions and offered latest technologies to India, as a special case. There was some opposition in the United States for offering this package to India but President Bush stood on his ground very firmly. Dr.Singh was naturally very much pleased with this offer. President Bush and Prime Minister Dr.Singh established good rapport. Dr Singh had all the praise for George Bush. The Communist Party of India was dead against this nuclear deal. At one point in time, it was felt that this deal would not go through the Indian parliament because Dr.Singh party was not in majority and it could have ended in a big fiasco and embarrassment to the whole country. Majority of Indians were in favor of this package but the Communists and other anti-Congress parties did not want this package approved by the parliament.

When Barack Obama became the President of the United States in 2008, he reversed many of the policies of George Bush. He almost took a U turn on U.S – China relations. He wanted to establish very special ties with Communist China. He paid a visit to China and was treated royally by the Chinese government. Obama was looking at Chinese friendship as leverage against the Russians. He also knew the financial clout that Chinese government has in the U.S economy. Billion of dollars worth of U.S treasury bonds had been purchased by the Chinese government. Naturally, it meant a lot in terms of financial stability of the U.S markets. Looking from that point of view, Obama was completely sold on China.

Obama was very much concerned at Pak/Afghan terrorist situation. Pakistan was very much eager to bring in Obama to the Kashmir problem. So when he appointed Holbrooke as his special envoy to Pak/Afghan issues, Pakistan requested that his envoy should also look into the Kashmir problem. Indian political observers were getting signals that Obama would be friendly with the

Chinese and soft with the Pakistanis. And that was troubling to the Indian government. Bush was highly in favor of India and was not interested in mediation efforts in Kashmir and he was not playing the China Card either. It was a challenge for the Indian Prime-Minister to change the Obama mindset.

Dr.Singh had to address these two important issues with President Obama when he was invited to visit United States. The background news was not encouraging to U.S-India relations. However, the meeting between Obama and Dr.Singh turned out to be very positive. A new setting was established for building friendly and mutually beneficial ties between the two countries. President Obama hosted a big dinner party in honor of the Prime-Minister. The credit for this very positive outcome has to be given to both leaders. This new reinforced chapter of Indo-U.S relations was a big relief to India. Many doubts about Obama China and Pakistan policies were cleared. In 2010, President Obama and first lady visited India and they were welcomed with great enthusiasm.

Let us look into our world political picture. The United States is the only Super Power at this junction. Russia has receded into a distant secondary position. Japan and Germany are no longer a military force. England and France are global powers-economically and militarily. However, it is the developing countries like China and India that are coming fast and would take up the center stage, in the world political arena, soon. China has become the second largest world economy, surpassing Japan. With a 5.4 trillions economy, China is far behind the United States economy of 15 trillions. China has the largest standing army in the world but there is no comparison with the United States in terms of nuclear heads and other sophisticated weapons of mass destruction. China does not have a single air craft carrier and its navy as well as its air force is no match to the United States. Compared to China, India is trailing far behind economically and militarily from China. With this background information, le us analyze the U.S-India future relations.

Foreign policies are spelled out on a short term basis and for the long run. How the United States would react under some potentially dangerous situations, it is difficult to predict. However, we can examine two important settings.

U.S POLICIES WHEN INDIA AND CHINA HAVE CONFLICT:

Let us consider setting number one when there is a conflict between India and China. Back in 1962, when China had invaded India, it was the United States that came to its rescue-not Russia. Since then, India and China had been talking with each other for the last forty years about their border dispute, but nothing tangible has come out so far. The Chinese and Indian leaders visit each other countries and tell the public that the world is big enough for both countries to move along with peace and prosperity; there is no reason to antagonize each other and create unnecessary problems. However, the general public in both countries distrust each other and do not believe that China and India could become close friends.

Sooner or later China is going to challenge the supremacy of the American influence in the Asian Peninsula. To counter balance the Chinese weight, the United States has to have some country like India, on its side.

The foreign policy planners in Washington should weigh these situations while formulating their policies towards India.

It seems very likely that China would not provoke India to take military actions against China; at the same time, it will not make any big concessions on border disputes. Both countries would keep on talking and come up with minor resolutions to the problems but at the end of the day nothing substantial is going to come out of all these publicized talks.

Relations between India and the United States are at their best, at this point in time. Obama and Dr.Singh have established good personal relations and there are similarities of views on Pak/Afghan terrorists, Taliban and Al Qaeda.

It has been observed that personal relations between head of the states carry a big weight in establishing closer ties between different countries. Kennedy, Bill Clinton, George Bush and now Obama have paid due attention to India and its place in the community of leading countries. From the Indian side, Prime-Minister Bajpai and Dr.Singh were instrumental in advancing the cause of Indo-American friendship.

There are more than one million Indians living in the United States. Americans are popular in India (unlike Pakistan); U.S.A is the leading democracy, India is the largest democracy. The biggest market for Indian Software /Services is the United States. The American dream is very much alive in India. With a population of 1.2 billions, about 250-300 million people of middle class society, India can be a real good ally of the United States.

In any global clash, Russia, China, Pakistan and Iran could take opposite side of the United States; whereas India, Japan and South Korea, most probably will go with the United States. This projection-for India, Japan and South Korea- will be good, when the future head of the states would continue to strengthen the existing friendly relations with the United States and vice-versa.

If there is a major clash between India and China, Pakistan and Russia might side with China; however, strong indications suggest that in that situation, United States would support India. (It is fervently hoped that the United States would not have Presidents like Nixon)

In order to avoid any confrontation with China, India does not provide any big help for the cause of Tibetan freedom. The Chinese rulers have destroyed the Tibetan culture and have made Tibet a slave country. The Dalai Lama, who lives in India, has made his best efforts to liberate his country peacefully from the clutches of Chinese rulers, has finally admitted that none of the western countries are willing to talk to China to make Tibet an autonomous state. If India and the United States make a pact to convince the Chinese government to grant freedom to Tibet, it would open a new chapter for global freedom.

India is the only country in Pacific Asia that could be a valuable asset to the United States, in any conflict. Japan military power-at this point-is negligible.

Considering all the existing conditions, it would be highly recommended that the United States should go out of its way to make India as one of the most trusted and reliable partners in this fast changing geo-political arena. It must be emphasized that India should be equally eager and forthcoming to take these relations to higher levels of trust and understanding. India needs a powerful and aspiring country like the United States for its future growth and prosperity as well as security. India has two potential adversaries-China and Pakistan. It must safeguard its freedom by selecting a country that has helped it in the past and it could do in the future.

U.S POLICIES WHEN INDIA AND PAKISTAN HAVE CONFLICTS:

Let us look into setting number two-a scenario when there is a war or serious clashes between India and Pakistan. What should be the policies of the United States in that situation-we have to address this question.

India and Pakistan have fought two full blown wars in 1965 and 1971. Indirectly, Pakistan has openly supported militants to cross the Line of Control (LOC) and create trouble in Indian Kashmir. This Kashmir dispute has been going on for the last sixty years. Pakistan wants American help-kind of mediation-to solve this ongoing issue. India on the other hand, does not want any third party mediation on Kashmir. Indian public does not want to give away any territory of Kashmir to Pakistan; on the other hand, Pakistani people claim that Kashmir belongs to them.

When Obama became President, he dropped hints that he would like to get Kashmir problem solved through U.S mediation. India conveyed very clearly that it does not want any kind of mediation from the United States. During the visit of Dr.Singh to the United States, this matter was finally resolved in favor of India. That was a big start for building a more solid foundation for India-U.S relations. Personal rapport between Obama and Dr.Singh produced a new opening for closer ties between India and the United States.

Al Qaeda, Taliban and Mujahedeen have taken a center stage of the United States foreign policy in Asia. Inspite of the fact that Bin Laden had been living in Pakistan for more than five years and Pakistan never gave any inkling of this to the United States, the government does not want to break relations with Pakistan. The reason is that Pakistan could create more troubles to the Americans and other western countries. The policy planners in Washington have to assess the implications of abandoning Pakistan. It is already a very good friend of China and it holds important connections to Afghan Taliban. The present stated policy of the United States that it encourages India and Pakistan to hold bilateral talks, is the best course of action at this juncture. Making India a crucial partner, would address many angles of regional security and zones of influence.

Trading and good business relations-in terms of import/export duties, preferential treatment, encouraging American companies to invest in India and providing nuclear reactors and other sophisticated military hardware will be good gestures on the part of the United States to further demonstrate the closeness of the relations with India.

India needs good paying jobs for its educated young working force. In this respect, the United State government should not oppose outsourcing to Indian Software companies. Further more the number of H1 Visas should be increased for Indian and other foreign students. These steps are bound to play a definite plus role in establishing close U.S-India relations.

Summing up the ramifications of the above mentioned political settings, it could be said with good degree of confidence that Kashmir dispute as well as India-China border dispute would remain on the discussion table for a long time before it become dead issues. The foreign policy of the United States towards India should be geared to a long term planning goal taking into stock the importance of the role that India can play for the benefit of the United States.

IMPORTANCE OF CLOSE RELATIONS BETWEEN U.S AND INDIA

The world supremacy of the United States would be challenged by Russia and China, individually or collectively. The internal stability of the country could face strong threats from countries like Pakistan, Afghanistan, Palestine and similar terrorist infested countries. India and England are in the same position as the United States is regarding terrorist game plan. It is important to look at the total picture when laying out policies for collaboration or active concern.

Russia and its allies could pose a threat to the United States and its western friends in Europe; China, down the road, may challenge the supremacy of the United States in Pacific and South East Asia.

The United States has military bases in Japan and South Korea. In any case of global or regional conflict, Australia, New Zeeland and Philippines would extend full support to the United States. If India, in such a case, extends its full support to the United States, it would really change the scene. In any conflict in Asia-may be over Taiwan or Tibet-it would be China that could precipitate troubles for the United States. In any conflict with China, Pakistan would support China and not the United States. In this context, the collaboration with India would carry a heavy weight.

Looking down the history pages, easy conclusion could be made regarding Japan and China; they can never be allies in any war. It is very true that countries of Asia would not like Japan to become a military giant because of its past history of aggression against China, Korea, Taiwan and other countries. The combined military strength of Australia, New Zeeland, Philippines and South Korea would be less than that of India. It clearly shows the importance of India connections.

War on terror, Al Qaeda and Taliban can not be waged by the United States, if Pakistan and Afghanistan do not co- operate with the United States. There are very strong indications that Pakistan might not support the efforts of the United States against terrorists. A week government in Afghanistan, with Taliban holding strong position, would act the same way as Pakistan would; that would mean duplicity in relations and giving away precious resources of money and equipment to these countries. The general public in both of these countries are anti-American and therefore should not be trusted by the United States policy planners. Once again, it would be India that would cooperate fully with the United States in the fight against religious fanatics and militants because it is facing the same enemy.

There could be many reasons for a country to be friendly with another one. United States and India have many common grounds to be close friends.

INDONESIA

Indonesia is a country of thousand of islands; the major ones are Sumatra, Java, Borneo and Bali. It is a country of great diversity, wonderful cultural heritage and natural beauty. It is the fourth largest populated country in the world with a population of two hundred forty millions strong. Java is the focal point of Indonesia; highly densely populated and a great cultural center.

From seventh Century to fourteen century, Sumatra and Java were part of Srivijay and Mjapahit kingdoms. They were Buddhist and Hindu empires. The Muslim religion was introduced by the Arab traders around fourteen century and presently, the country is 86% Muslim. Indonesia is a secular nation; it is founded on five principles: Monotheism, Humanitarianism, National Unity, Representative Democracy and Social Justice. They are called Panchsheel.

Indonesia became Dutch East Indies under Dutch rule-from Sixteen to Nineteen Century. During the World War II, Japan had the control over Indonesia. The Indonesians were so disgusted with the Dutch rulers that they welcomed the Japanese as their liberators. On 17th August 1945, nationalist leader Soekarno declared Republic of Indonesia as a free nation. However, the Dutch government did not want to grant freedom to Indonesia; it was the United States that exerted political pressure on the Dutch to leave Indonesia and finally in 1949, Indonesia joined the United Nations as a free country.

As a free nation, Indonesia along with India started Non Aligned Movement and followed Socialistic policies in governing their countries. During sixties, Indonesia was facing problems in terms of economic growth and general stability as a nation. In 1966, President Soekarno was replaced by General Suharto as the new President of the country. General Suharto was instrumental in transforming an agricultural economy to a flourishing industrial society. At the same time, the authoritarian rule of General Suharto brought corruption to all levels of governance. The country as a result suffered tremendously because of these corrupt practices. The general public finally got rid of General Suharto in 1998 after thirty two years of his presidency.

One of the most tragic events happened in 2004 when an earthquake rattled under the sea near the north province of Sumatra-Banda Achae. It triggered massive Tsunami waves hitting Indonesia, Thailand, India and Ceylon. More than 250,000 people died; 155,000 people in Indonesia lost their lives. Loss of property was in billions. The whole world rose to the occasion.

The first democratically held election for the presidency of Indonesia took place in 2004. The former military general of Indonesian army, General Susilo Yudhoyono was elected as the President, defeating Ms Sukarnoputri, the daughter of the first President Soekarno. President Yudhoyono has been elected for his second term in 2009. Indonesia needs top leaders to eradicate corruption which is crippling the whole governing system. So far, the President has succeeded in this direction to some extent. The rate of growth is around 6%. People are hoping that he would be able to bring prosperity and better times if he keeps his promises and keep on bringing large amount of foreign investments to the country. Luckily Indonesia is not a favorite country for Islamic Militants; there are, however, isolate cases of bombing and anti-western agitation.

Structural Foundations Analysis

All developing countries have to cross certain hurdles before they reach a take off stage in their progression. Corruption, lack of governing expertise, no clear cut goals, unsatisfactory infra structure, low education standards, poor health care, shortage of business know how and type of governing system play very important role in reaching this point of inflection. Let us look at the present prevailing conditions in Indonesia and compare them with those of other Asian countries like China, India, South Korea and Malaysia.

Malaysia and Indonesia have some important common connections. Bahasa Indonesia is very similar to Malaysian language, spoken by most of the Muslim population of Malaysia. Both countries have majority of Muslim population. The island of Borneo is split between Indonesia and Malaysia. During 7th Century A.D and extending further on, both countries were ruled by Hindu and Buddhist rulers. But there are stark differences too. Whereas Malaysia came under the British rule, Indonesia was governed by the Dutch. The imperialist rulers were interested in their own prosperity and well being, no doubt about it. However, there were differences between British governing system and the Dutch. The Dutch made no improvement during their three hundred years of rule in the country; however, the British did something to modernize, in some ways, the governing structure and thinking of Malaysian society. These differences made big impact in terms of structural foundations for Malaysia and Indonesia. Similarly, more than two hundred years of British Raj, gave India the benefit of thriving and proactive British practices to the Indian society.

Malaysia has a very small population of 28 millions compared to Indonesian 230 millions strong. National Income for a Malaysian is around $8,000 compared to $4,000 for an Indonesian. Malaysia is ahead of Indonesia in terms of better healthcare for the ordinary citizen, better job opportunities, better infra structure for establishing global businesses, higher education standards, more democratic and transparent government and far less corruption. Malaysia has the advantage of having a very energetic Chinese community that is instrumental in starting new enterprises and thus creating more national wealth. The rate of growth for both countries is between 5-6%. The large population of Indonesia has some pluses and some negative features. Strong leadership, higher business growth, non corrupt governing structure could put Indonesia ahead of Malaysia in terms of Gross Domestic Product.

South Korea is standing just behind China, Japan and India. It seems difficult for Indonesia and Malaysia to overtake it. Few decades ago, South Korea was undergoing the same phase of overall growth and expansion as Indonesia and Malaysia are going through now. At this point, it really has made tremendous strides when we examine its economy, standard of living and well being of an ordinary citizen. The Gross National Income per capita is around $16,000 and the Gross Domestic Product is growing steadily.

India and China are two outstanding developing countries that would be counted as great economic and political powers of the world, in the very near future. With the available information, we can say with surety that South Korea, Indonesia and Malaysia are on the right track for a great take off.

Political Relations with Other countries

Developing countries have to select those nations as their best friends who could invest and support their goals and objectives. It is applicable to Indonesia as well. Three hundred years of Dutch rule created animosity towards the ruling nation.The net result of this unfriendly relation is that very few Dutch companies operate in Indonesia. In reality Indonesia does not have any European country that could be termed as special and close to the nation. However, normal friendly relations exist between Indonesia and other European countries but nothing more. However, in Asia, Indonesia has established special trading partners. As a founding member of ASEAN and OPEC, it is playing its role effectively. Free trading agreements have been signed with some Asian countries.

Japan is the biggest investor and trading partner in Indonesia, followed by Australia, China, Singapore and South Korea. Indonesia, at this stage of development needs a steady, progressive economic growth that would entitle it political influence in the region. Down the road it could start building a military base to support its global recognition.

Indonesia is one of the founding members of Non Aligned Movement. Presently, it has a membership of around fifty member countries, through out Asia and Africa. In the current global politics, Non Aligned Movement does not carry any weight but it has a significant affect on building common grounds for friendship, peace and stability amongst different countries specially the developing countries have a united front to voice its concerns against the powerful countries of the world. In this respect, India, China and Indonesia represent a united front. On a political level, Indonesia has established good friendly relations with India, China, Malaysia, Japan, United States and South Korea.

At this juncture in history, Indonesia is standing at the crossroad of dramatic improvement or stagnation. The country could go in either direction depending upon the platform of efficiency, constant efforts and strong leadership versus rampant corruption, incompetent governing structure and lack of clearly defined goals and objective3s. Indonesia is such a diverse country with so many different dialects, traditions, cultural heritage that it really requires a powerful personality that is acceptable to all sections of the society; a mediocre would not be able to carry the weight of this tremendous responsibility.

Among the countries that could make significant difference for prosperity and higher economical growth for Indonesia, Japan, United States, Australia, India and China could be counted as the most important ones. The Indonesian government should establish good political relations with these countries in order to get the best results. During the time when General Suharto was the President of Indonesia, many of these countries were by passed and on top of this omission, corruption was raging high at the highest level with the result that Indonesia started going down the hill and there was outrage at the failures of the governing leadership. The present President of Indonesia Susilo Yudhoyono is turning the corners and it may pick up good rate of growth during his presidency. Only time would show how much he can achieve in his second term.

When we look at different countries of Asia, there are some which have not reached the Take Off stage of the economy. Philippines, Sri Lanka, Burma and Viet Nam are still struggling. Thailand, Indonesia and Malaysia are on the right track but there are many important factors that would govern the final outcome. Most of these countries have export oriented economy and when there is global recession, their growth slows down, too.

United States has a big stake in what happens in Indonesia. Back in 2008, President Yudhoyono wanted to establish a Comprehensive Partnership Program with U.S.A. To achieve this goal, Secretary of State, Hillary Clinton visited Indonesia in 2009 and signed the documents to start this program. Many projects have been selected in the areas of Agriculture, Education, Health Care and Military Training under USAID program. In 2010, President Obama visited Indonesia and expressed his full support for Comprehensive Partnership Treaty.

In this changing world, all aspects of foreign policy have to be examined and reassessed from time to time. It is a good bet that within few decades, China would challenge the United States in many fronts. To counter this threat, U.S.A has to find good allies to support its goals and objectives. Indonesia as a fast coming up country could be a good choice. With a large population of 230 million people and an organized military force, Indonesia like South Korea could be counted as a reliable ally. After the Iraqi War, most of the Muslim countries of the world have gone against the United States and its policies. Indonesia is the most populated Muslim country; having good relations with it means a rebuttal to many Muslim countries. On the other hand, it is good for

Indonesia to have United States as its partner. It might help the country to achieve higher economic growth and all round progress in all areas of Education, Agriculture, Military Strength and Health Care. To have India, Indonesia, Australia and Japan on its side United States would be able to build a strong force against China and Russia.

Indonesia can take a good lead in establishing strong economical and political relations with Turkey, a secular and westernized country. At this juncture Turkey is ahead of Indonesia in all aspects-Education, Health Care, Infra Structure, Transparent Governing System, peace and stability. Together with Malaysia, Indonesia and Turkey can change the climate of animosity and misunderstanding between the Muslim countries and the western countries specially the United States. Radicalization, Extremism and non tolerance have become important features of the Muslim world, these days. It is a dangerous trend and has to be curbed and eliminated for the welfare of the whole world.

It is good to see that Indonesia is unlike Afghanistan, Pakistan and Iran; all these three Muslim countries have become source of concern for the welfare of the whole world. If Indonesia can mold the attitude and policy making apparatus of the Muslim countries which are members of Islamic Countries Organization, it will do a commendable service to the rest of the world. Associations based purely on religious grounds can do more harm than harmony to the world.

MALAYSIA

Malaysia gained its independence from Britain in 1957. Singapore once a part of Federation of Malaysia became an independent country in 1963.The present population of the country-year 2010- is 28 millions. 54% population is Malays, 26% are local Chinese and 8% are Indians. The Chinese are the richest; they run the business. Malays run the government and Indians form the bottom ladder of the society. The Gross Domestic Product is 255 Billions; the rate of growth is around 6%. The Gross National Income is $8,000 per capita. According to Asian standard, Malaysia is a well to do country. Japan, Singapore and South Korea are ahead of Malaysia in terms of standard of living.

The most influential leader of Malaysia happened to be Dr.Mahathir Mohamed who ruled the country for twenty two years -1981to2003. Dr. Mahathir should be given full credit for transforming a backward country to a highly advanced economy. He was not an admirer of the United States; during Asian Economic problems in 1997, he openly criticized the western countries for currency exchange turmoil. When his deputy, Anwar Ibrahim opposed him for his views on the western countries, he sacked him and made charges of corruption and sexual misconduct, sodomy against him. Mr. Ibrahim was sentenced to a jail term of six years. In 2009, National Front Coalition party elected Najib Abdul Razak as the new Prime-Minister of Malaysia replacing Mr.Badawi who had resigned in the wake of election losses of his party, the

National Front. The National Front Coalition Party is the largest political party of Malaysia; Dr.Mahathir was one of the founders of National Front and he still holds lot of political influence in the country.

Malaysia is a large producer of Liquid Petroleum Gas, Palm oil and is one of the largest manufacturers of computer products. United States is the largest investor in the country. The leading trading partners are China, Singapore, Japan, Unites States and Indonesia. In 2007, United States declined to sign Free Trade Treaty with Malaysia. However, United States is providing assistance in many areas of health care, advanced education and military training to the country. In terms of industrialization, technical know how and business environment, Malaysia is behind South Korea.

Malaysia's diverse society consisting of ethnic Malays, Chinese and Indians has not integrated into a melting pot. The official policy of positive discrimination in favor of local Malays has generated ill will among different sections of the society. The present Prime Minister Najib Razak has outlined a policy to gradual removal of this favoritism towards Malays who are called Bhoomiputra-the sons of the soil. It is interesting to note that many words in Malaysian and Indonesian languages are of Indian origin. Sixty percent population of Malaysia is Muslim; about twenty five percent are Buddhist and Hindus and the rest are Christians. It is a moderate Muslim country.

Problems and Opportunities

Since its independence, Malaysia has become a roaring tiger of East Asia. After 1997, the economy has slowed down but still inching towards higher grounds. The leadership of the country should move towards improving overall higher educational standards, better health care for the general public, transparency in governance, addressing corruption at different levels and removing favorable discrimination for ethnic Malays in all areas of the government. All citizens of the country should be treated on an equal footing .There are strong laws which prohibit free expression against the government. And there are many cases of Human Rights Violations; people are put in jails without trials and equality of all citizens before judicial courts is in question. The government has failed to integrate the different sections of the society into a homogenous mold. These are serious problems for the country that have to be addressed sooner than later because it is going to blunt the upward progress of the country.

Malaysia needs a strong army and military power to exercise its influence in regional politics. It is founding member of ASEAN-Association of South East Asian Nations and OIC-Organization of Islamic Countries. If Malaysian leaders follow the Turkish model of secularism, it would propel the country towards progressive global trends. Religion should be separated from governing and formulating the country's international policies. Countries which are forged based on religion carry a heavy baggage of old history.

There are huge opportunities lying before Malaysia. It has laid solid structure for moving forward. The country could achieve dramatic results in terms of prosperity and well being of its citizens if concrete measures are being taken by the leaders of the country. It is very true that leaders can guide a nation in the right direction provided they are sincere and honest and carry the general public with them with their plans and programs. Corruption, delays in decision making and not sure about the outcome, would hamper the path of genuine progress .For every thing to click, continuous efforts have to be made in the field of education, technical know how, business savvy environment, stability and peace in the country. Malaysia is endowed with natural resources and with clear cut goals it can reach the prosperity standards of South Korea in a short period of time.

It is very important to note that the Muslim community of the country does not support extreme Islamic teachings. There are Hindus, Buddhists and Christians living side by side as neighbors and they have the freedom to follow their own religions. This scenario does not exists in many Muslim countries and this is a very good sign for any country.

At this point in time, Malaysia does not have to be afraid of its military generals. They are not powerful to replace a democratically elected government. Most likely, this trend would continue in the future and the country would move forward as a genuine democracy. We see a bright future for the country unless the politicians and the leaders of the society move in the wrong directions. Like many developing countries of Asia, Malaysia needs honest, dedicated and bold leaders at the highest places of governance; corruption and self interests would become the stumbling block and the country would be stuck in the zero progress zone. This has happened in quite a few countries of Asia and Africa.

Relations with other countries

The immediate neighbor of Malaysia is Indonesia; there are many facets which are common to both countries. Both are Muslim countries; Indonesian language-Bhasa-has common roots with the ethnic Malay's language. However, there are stark differences between two countries. Malaysia is ahead of Indonesia in terms of Educational standards, health care facilities, Gross Domestic Product, National Income per capita and rate of growth. Whereas Malaysia has three major subdivisions of the society, Indonesia has a very wide diverse population with many local languages and different social and cultural differences .There is a large community of Indonesians who work in Malaysia. Both countries are active members of ASEAN and OIC, but there is no military treaty between them. Malaysia and Indonesia, at this juncture are good friends.

India and Malaysia have friendly relations though off and on local Indians have complained of serious problems of discrimination against them. The present Prime-Minister of Malaysia Najib Razak has promised to do away with the existing laws of providing special quota of jobs and other assistance programs exclusively to Muslim Malays. So far, no big progress has been achieved in this area. India is in a position to help Malaysia in providing advanced military training to its officers; it can help also in other areas like health care and advanced technical know how. India and Malaysia do not have Free Trade Agreement and do not have any military alliance.

More than 26% of Malaysian population has Chinese ancestry. They have been instrumental in transforming Malaysia into a vibrant country. The business community has established good connections with Singapore, Taiwan and China. Ironically, the Chinese community has few political and social leaders on the national scale and that is delaying the removal of discriminatory policies against the minority community. The Malaysian Chinese would not associate with the mainland Chinese; he would rather prefer a Taiwanese. There is no military cooperation between China and Malaysia. The Peoples Republic of China is not interested in meddling in the internal politics of Malaysia at this crossroad. Only the future would tell how much influence mainland China would like to exert on Malaysia down the road.

As mentioned above, Malaysia and the United States have maintained friendly relations. Many American companies have invested heavily in Malaysian manufacturing and Gas utilities. The United States is number one investor in the country. It is providing assistance in many other areas like education, health care, military training, research and development and technical fields. It should be noted however that both countries could not be termed as close allies. In the past, Dr.Mahathir used to deliver anti-U.S speeches whenever he had some disagreement with the United States policies. There is no Free Trade Agreement and there is no military pact between the two countries. Looking from a broad perspective of China's rise in the East, United States has to weigh its position and count its friends in case something goes wrong in that part of the world. The current political image of the United States in Malaysia is not very favorable but it is not very anti either. Based on this assumption, United States should start making moves to bring Malaysia into its orbit.

Extreme Islam

Khomeni's Iranian revolution has left a lasting influence in the Muslim world. It has awakened some deep rooted thoughts among many people especially young women. Higab, the head scarf, has become a symbol of Muslim womanhood. Like in other countries, Malaysian women are going for it and are advocating strict Islamic customs and traditions. The Malaysian government however has remained neutral on this issue. There are some people who want Muslim Sharia rules to be applied universally throughout the country. Extreme western trends in dress and culture are not popular; in fact they are considered outrageous. This trend of adopting strict Muslim ways of every day living would have divisive affect on the society. Many European countries have taken a firm stand against this phenomenon. In Asia, old and new ways would continue to prevail. The majority of Muslim Malaysians are moderate in their views of life and most probably, it would not affect the national fabric of tolerance and accommodation for other religions. Very recently the word Allaha could not be used by non Muslims when referring to God; luckily, the highest court of Malaysia ruled that this word is not the monopoly of Muslims. Conversion of any Muslim to any other religion is considered illegal in Malaysia. In some ways, Muslim Malaysians have to think what individual freedom mean to them.

Discrimination against the minorities-Chinese and Indians-in terms of scholarship, good jobs, housing etc has forced many people to migrate to other countries. It is reported that about a million people in the recent past have left Malaysia because the government policies and rules discouraged them to stay in the country. These very people could have created lot of jobs for other Malaysians and would have contributed towards growth and prosperity for the country. The local ethnic Malaysian people occupy the most important positions in the government but somehow have not shown very promising signs in business ventures. It is the Chinese who are doing very good in this area and are bringing wealth and prosperity to the country.

More than fifty years have gone by since Malaysia got its independence, yet there is no melting pot in the society. Chinese stays with Chinese, Indians go along with Indians and local Muslims remain Muslim- there is hardly any kind of integration between these three groups of people. This scenario is not good for the country as a whole. If Malaysians look towards United States, they can learn a very encouraging lesson of cohesiveness, enrichment of different cultures and a common denominator of love for the country. The sea of integration is more powerful than the wall of isolation and self centered ideas.

Malaysia has to embark upon modern and secular ways of conducting its business. Religion has hampered progress in the history of countries, most of the time. Developing Asian countries should learn from secular western countries to keep religion separate from the state business.

Looking from global political point of view, Malaysia is not likely to fall into Peoples Republic of China's shadow .The relations with Russia and China would be friendly but not very cozy, as it seems at this point in time. We see better overall relations with the United States. Strategically, United States has to take some important steps to establish stronger friendly relations.

UNSTABLE

Afghanistan and Pakistan are two countries that have received billions of aid from the United States as well as from other countries and international financial institutions for one reason and it was to wipe out Afghan and Pak Taliban militants. But it did not happen; they are thriving well and are causing lot of headache to the NATO and American troops. These very Taliban fighters were responsible to drive out the mighty Russian army brigades from Afghans soil. These militants are in fact freedom fighters and they do not want any foreigners to occupy their land. President Obama has made a correct policy to withdraw the American forces by 2014 from Afghanistan and let the Afghan people take control of their country themselves. There is no need to spill unnecessary blood for a cause which is very difficult to achieve. The best policy for the United States and NATO countries is to provide military training and armaments to the Afghan army and let them do the fighting against the Taliban.

Taliban fighters would be willing to make a truce with the United States once they come to realize that Americans would be leaving, sooner or later and they could prevail once again as they did before 2001.On the other hand, this time President Karzai political party would be in a stronger position to negotiate a better and favorable peace treaty with the Taliban. At this moment, United States and Taliban are talking and by 2014, there might be some kind of mutual peaceful agreement between the two parties which perhaps would be the best solution to this thorny situation. However, this coalition between Taliban and the Afghan political parties would be uncertain and unstable. It might take a few decades before the two opposing group start doing something constructive and helpful to move the country forward. The future still remains bleak and unpredictable. Afghan citizens have suffered a lot in the past and should be helped by the International community.

Corruption, illiteracy, poverty and old religious values have kept Pakistan in a dangerous situation. Al-Quaeda and Pakistani religious organizations have made the Pakistan's government ineffective and in a way helpless. Militants roam in the city and get their way with out any fear or police punishment. The economy is going down the hill; the inflation is high and there is no government rule or regulation to catch the thief. United States has provided a handsome aid of two billion dollars a year, to the Pakistan government for the last ten years or so. The results have been disappointing so far. Pakistan has become a good breeding ground for all kind of Jihadis or Militants. To the surprise of the whole world, it was Pakistan where Osama Bin Laden had been living for more than six years before he was killed by the U.S commandos in 2011. Because Afghanistan is a land locked country, all the military supplies of the U.S army had to pass through Pakistan territory; logistically Pakistan has a strategic advantage .Just for that reason, Pakistan has been provided with lot of money to keep the supplies flowing. The Pakistan military establishment is very strong and the newly elected government headed by Prime-Minister Asif Zardari is afraid of a military coup; no body knows when that can happen. The government is standing on a shaky ground. At the moment, Pakistan has become a failed state

AFGHANISTAN

One of the most dangerous places on this earth is Afghanistan. It is also one of the poorest countries in the world. The life expectancy is less than fifty years. Eighty percent of heroin crop is grown in Afghanistan. Illiteracy and unemployment hovers around seventy percent. No wonder it is a fertile ground for terrorists, militants, Taliban and Al-Qaeda.

Afghan citizens have suffered tremendously during the last two decades spanning through 1979 to 2000. When the Russians had occupied Afghanistan, militant Mujahedeen and Taliban militia men fought against the Russians and ultimately they became the ruler of the country. Taliban war lords created havoc in the country. They followed strict Sharia laws; provided shelter and support to Al Qaeda leaders-Bin Laden and his deputy Al Zarahiri.(Bin Laden is now dead)

After 9/11, American forces, invaded Afghanistan and within a short span of time, routed the Taliban regime. Dr Hamid Karzai became the President of the country. It was not an easy task for President Karzai to bring back Afghanistan to a normal state. Taliban and Al Qaeda militants were still roaming around the country side; drug lords were controlling the city streets. Corruption was rampant; there was no rule of law. The general public was under the mercy of illiterate, religious fanatics who knew nothing except Koran.

When the elections were held to select the President, Taliban created trouble. Allegations of rigged election were made. United States had no choice but to accept the verdict of the so called fair election. President Karzai, once again became the head of the state. Political pressure was exerted on the President to clean up the state of the affairs related to corruption and drug trafficking. However, the progress in this direction was very slow and no tangible result was forthcoming.

In the mean time the Taliban militants were regrouping to attack the Afghan government. The United States army along with the United Nation forces could not eliminate the Taliban. They are still very well entrenched in the mountain caves and are ready to fight again. We must not forget that the Afghan War is not a regular war-it is a Guerilla War just like the Viet Nam War. The Taliban forces have the tactical advantage which the United States does not have. They know their territory very thoroughly; they know where to run to save themselves-in the caves. The United States and the western powers should learn the lessons from the Viet Nam War. The alternative could lead to disastrous results.

If we look back at the history of Mujahedeen, Taliban and Al Qaeda in Afghanistan, it is very clear that the local people do favor these groups, in some way or the other. They were not happy with the Russians AND THEY FEEL THAT the Americans, like wise, should leave them alone to decide their future. Taking this important aspect of Afghanistan point of view, the current and the near future policies should be geared to address this situation.

Mujahedeen-the freedom fighters-and Taliban-the students of Islamic Schools were nurtured in Pakistan.. The Pakistan army trained these people; I.S.I-the Pakistan's intelligence agency provided all the technical know how to these militants. With the help of Al Qaeda, Taliban is now fighting the Americans.

Taliban is split into two groups-Afghan Taliban and Pakistan's Taliban. Omar Abdullah is the head of Afghan's Taliban and Al Mehsud is the top dog of Pakistan's terrorist organization. Pakistan had maintained good connections with the Afghan's Taliban group, in the past. Some intelligent sources say that I.S.I does have solid relation with Afghans Taliban even today. General Petraeus, Commander of NATO International Security Forces has recently stated that this is the core problem between Pakistan and the United States.

Recently, President Obama made a policy statement on Afghanistan outlining the future actions to be taken by the United States. The most important point that he made was that the United States would start withdrawing the army personnel beginning from July 2011 and the total withdrawal would be completed by 2014. The Afghan army, by that time should be able to take control of the safety and well being of the Afghan citizens. The American army and the NATO Security Forces are building a modern fighting force to safeguard the freedom of the Afghan country. It is hoped that this army would overwhelm the enemies of the country namely Taliban and Al Qaeda.

Knowing these facts, the Pakistan government is trying to establish a plateau of influence in Kabul, once the American forces leave the country. Pakistan's Intelligence agency-I.S.I- friendly relations with Afghan's Taliban could play an important role in implementing this strategy. Furthermore, Pakistan wants to minimize the influence of India in the future set up of the Afghanistan government

ROLE OF RELIGION, POVERTY AND MILITARY FORCE

Religion plays a very important role in any society. It is very true in Muslim countries. It has been observed that level of education and monetary position of the individual or the family somehow dictates the orientation and behavior towards religion. Afghanistan has very high illiteracy and it is a very poor country. There is no thriving industry; farmers are destitute-they have no choice but to grow heroin plants to make some money. Under these circumstances, the general public has become highly religious. Unfortunately, Afghan Taliban took control over the country and started implementing strict rules and regulations of the Muslim legal laws called Sharia. Under these rules, a woman can not go to school; she is not allowed to go out of home without a full veil called Burka. Sharia laws have relegated women to slavery. Brutal and inhuman means are employed to punish the offenders.

When we look at most of the Muslim countries of the world, we find some common denominators. Majority of the people, in these countries are poor, there is very little industrialization which means high unemployment. Illiteracy is rampant; modern government structure and institutions are missing. Very little of technical know how is available; people have no idea where the world is heading to. There is very thin slice of the middle class existing in these countries. Exceptions are there but these attributes are statistically correct. No One of the most dangerous places on this earth is Afghanistan. It is also one of the poorest countries in the world. The life expectancy is less than fifty years. Eighty percent of heroin crop is grown in Afghanistan. Illiteracy and unemployment hovers around seventy percent. No wonder

Afghan citizens have suffered tremendously during the last two decades spanning through 1979 to 2000. When the Russians had occupied Afghanistan, militant Mujahedeen and Taliban militia men fought against the Russians and ultimately they became the ruler of the it is a fertile ground for terrorists, militants, Taliban and Al-Qaeda.country. Taliban war lords created havoc in the country. They followed strict Sharia laws; provided shelter and support to Al Qaeda leaders-Bin Laden and his deputy Al Zarahiri.(Bin Laden is now dead)

After 9/11, American forces, invaded Afghanistan and within a short span of time, routed the Taliban regime. Dr Hamid Karzai became the President of the country. It was not an easy task for President Karzai to bring back Afghanistan to a normal state. Taliban and Al Qaeda militants were still roaming around the country side; drug lords were controlling the city streets. Corruption was rampant; there was no rule of law. The general public was under the mercy of illiterate, religious fanatics who knew nothing except Koran.

When the elections were held to select the President, Taliban created trouble. Allegations of rigged election were made. United States had no choice but to accept the verdict of the so called fair election. President Karzai, once again became the head of the state. Political pressure was exerted on the President to clean up the state of the affairs related to corruption and drug trafficking. However, the progress in this direction was very slow and no tangible result was forthcoming.

In the mean time the Taliban militants were regrouping to attack the Afghan government. The United States army along with the United Nation forces could not eliminate the Taliban. They are still very well entrenched in the mountain caves and are ready to fight again. We must not forget that the Afghan War is not a regular war-it is a Guerilla War just like the Viet Nam War. The Taliban forces have the tactical advantage which the United States does not have. They know their territory very thoroughly; they know where to run to save themselves-in the caves. The United States and the western powers should learn the lessons from the Viet Nam War. The alternative could lead to disastrous results.

If we look back at the history of Mujahedeen, Taliban and Al Qaeda in Afghanistan, it is very clear that the local people do favor these groups, in some way or the other. They were not happy with the Russians and they feel that the Americans, like wise, should leave them alone to decide their future. Taking this important aspect of Afghanistan point of view, the current and the near future policies should be geared to address this situation.

Mujahedeen-the freedom fighters-and Taliban-the students of Islamic Schools were trained and nurtured in Pakistan. The governments of Saudi Arabia and the United States provided the necessary funds to these militants group. The objective at that time was to drive out the Russians from Afghanistan. Pakistan has become the breeding grounds of religious fanatics and Suicide bombers.

Let us examine some aspects of Islam-the Muslim religion. Wrong or right, it has been said that this religion was spread by the force of sword-not by love. There are two important words in Koran-the holy book of Muslims-Faithful and Infidel; either you are my soul brother or you are my enemy-there is no in between. Tolerance for other faiths and beliefs are hard to find. A Muslim by birth would always remain a Muslim-he/she can not change his/her religion. If any body is bold enough to defy this law, punishment would be severe. A Muslim person can not marry a non Muslim; he/she has to convert to become Muslim. No body can criticize Muslim Prophet; there is no room for it.

It is very difficult to change a culture, its core values and beliefs. It is not impossible but it takes a long time. To bring Afghanistan from its present state of affairs to the twenty first century norms would require tremendous resources and determination. Religion would be a big hurdle; it would not be easy. Sending girls to school, allowing women to work outside of their home, watching movies or following western culture traits and characteristics-all of these and other similar things would block the transformation of the Afghan society for a long time to come.

United States and other western countries have spent lot of money and have made huge sacrifices in terms of losses of human lives to defeat Al Qaeda and Taliban. The strategy to follow in this situation should be, not to offend the Afghan people beliefs and traditions. The citizens of Afghanistan have suffered a lot during these twenty years or more. They are not looking for a Marshal Plan but they do want some kind of generosity from the United States to live safely.

Poverty

Poverty breeds hatred, revenge, irrationality and ultimately militancy. Suicide bombers are born in this environment. When a person goes hungry day after day, he either dies of starvation or become a recruit for rebellion. Like many other countries of the world, Afghanistan is passing through this crisis. This situation is the resultant affect of incompetent leadership of the country as well as many other factors.

Right now, Afghanistan is facing not only wide spread poverty but it is surrounded by uneducated fanatic members of Taliban and Al Qaeda. For the last eight years, American forces are trying to eliminate these militants but they have not been successful as of now. As pointed out before, war in Afghanistan is not a regular warfare-it is a hit and run guerilla war. Prevailing conditions in the country forces the young and adult to join the militants. This way they are assured of food and other amenities.

United States and other western countries have to address this question of poverty in order to succeed in their objective of defeating the Taliban and Al Qaeda. It is very true that food program sponsored by the United Nations have failed to stop the poverty in any country. The solution to this problem is to provide education, technical training, and setting up pockets of industrialization and create jobs. If the country is at its feet, the problem of poverty would start going down. That requires resources –money, personnel, expertise, devotion and patience. Things won't change overnight-it will take some time to bloom.

In most of the cases, attacking poverty starts with agriculture production. Providing good seeds, fertilizer and modern machinery like tractors, insecticide and reliable irrigation system would immediately make the impact on the poverty level. A nation which can feed itself would never become a safe haven for terrorists and militants. It is true that when the country is fighting an active war, it becomes difficult to divert attention towards other activities like increasing productivity in agriculture or setting up manufacturing units or even opening new schools for training. In a situation like this, the government should continue to take baby steps and when the right moment comes in, move with vigor and speed.

Afghan people are known for their freedom loving nature; they are skilled fighters-resolute and courageous. They do not like to be governed by outsiders. For a long time, Afghanistan had been known for their independence, their unique culture-not grounded in modern professional skills. Universal education had been missing and industrialization was almost negligible. In this twenty first century, countries with such characteristics find it difficult to move on with the rest of the world. It is up to national leaders to take up this challenge of uplifting their countries and make their fellow citizens happy and well nourished.

When a foreign policy is laid down on a table, short term and long term planning has to be spelled out precisely. Under the present conditions in Afghanistan, the short term goals for the United States would be directed towards the crushing defeat of militants. The long term objectives should be to bring stability and prosperity to the citizens of Afghanistan. Education, social and economical advancement, better job opportunities should be top priorities.

Military Force

After almost ten years, Bin Laden was found hiding in Pakistan; he was shot dead by the American Commando team on May 2011. It was a great day for America. However, the death of Bin Laden does not mean the end of Taliban and other terrorists groups. Haqqini militants and Afghan Taliban are very well entrenched on the borders of Pakistan and Afghanistan. They are well trained-most probably by the Pakistan army-and are ready to die for Islamic Jihad. These Islamic fighters are good in guerilla war tactics and they know the territory very well unlike the American and western military personnel. We must also remember that these Jihadists are coming from poverty driven families and have nothing to lose except their own life.

The socio-economical conditions dictate that it would be impossible to wipe out Taliban and Al Qaeda from Afghanistan and Pakistan. However, the responsibility to defeat these elements should be entrusted to the local people. It does not make any sense to expose American soldiers to death traps; let the Afghan army personnel handle their own people-kill the terrorists and suicide bombers. They would be able to do a good job provided they are given proper training and fighting equipment.

President Obama had outlined his withdrawal policy from Afghanistan starting from July 2011. Now, Bin Laden has gone, Al Qaeda and Taliban could be defeated without increasing the army personnel from the United States. Further more, the time table for withdrawal could be expedited-instead of 2014 final withdrawal, make it 2013. It is imperative that Afghan's forces be well trained and well equipped with military hardware. It must also be made clear to Pakistan that it should stop all kinds of help to Afghan's Taliban and other militants group. In the past, Pakistan has been involved directly or indirectly in providing military training to Afghan's Taliban and it had kept good relations with Haqqini militants. There are thousands of Afghan families who are living in Pakistan and they constitute potential recruits.

Waziristan-north western province of Pakistan-and other hilly regions on the border have been providing shelter and safety net to the members of Al Qaeda and Taliban and Pakistan army could do nothing or say was not willing to take any risk against these terrorists. It is not in the interest of Pakistan to antagonize these militants group. For the namesake, Pakistan government has been assuring the U.S that the backbone of these outfits has been broken but in reality, it is providing a safe haven to Al Qaeda,Taliban,LeT and other terror groups. . These organizations could be utilized against U.S and India, if the need arise. American military and foreign policy architects should make a note of it.

Massive military aid to Afghanistan would not change the over all picture in the country. It is a combination of Economic, technical, health and other related assistance that is needed the most. Poverty, illiteracy, poor health and old religious views take a long time to correct. If the United States and other countries want to see a prosperous and vigilant Afghanistan, they should be ready to invest in many areas of the modern day living. This country needs lot of help before it can stand on its own feet

.

PAKISTAN

Pakistan is the only Muslim country which has weapons of mass destruction-it is a full fledged nuclear state. Nawaz Sharif was the Prime-Minister of Pakistan when it became the member of this exclusive club, back in 1998. This happened when India too, successfully tested its nuclear technology. President Bill Clinton reacted sharply and he imposed sanctions against both countries. In 1947 the British government had partitioned the country into two independent states-India and Pakistan. Right from day one, both countries have become arch enemies and both are nuclear powers.

In 1979, Russian forces had invaded Afghanistan-some people say that the Russians had come, at the invitation of the Prime Minister of Afghanistan. The American reaction was swift and forceful. Pakistan was made a strategic partner in driving out the Russians from Afghanistan. With the help of Saudi Arabia and Pakistan army, Russians had to leave Afghanistan in 1989. In this process, the freedom fighters –the Mujahedeen-and Taliban-the students from Islamic schools called Madrassas, came into existence. These two groups were provided with arms and military training by the United States and Pakistan Intelligence Agency.

India and Pakistan had fought two wars against each other -1965 and 1971-over the dispute of Kashmir. In 1997, the Commander in chief of Pakistan who happened to be Parvez Musharaff, ordered his troops to go into Indian territory and started a surprise attack on Indian forces in Kargil. Many Indian soldiers were killed. This action from the commander in chief was taken without informing the Prime Minister of Pakistan Nawaz Sharif. He was furious; he might have thought of replacing Musharaff. In 1999, Musharaff staged a blood less coup and toppled the government of Nawaz Sharif and sent him to exile in Saudia Arabia.

In the mean time, Taliban and Mujahedeen had defeated the Russians; disposed off the Afghan monarchy and declared themselves as the ruler of the country. Pakistan and Saudi Arabia recognized the new rulers of Afghanistan as the lawful government. Taliban government extended full support to Al Qaeda and Bin Laden. Pakistan intelligence agency was keeping good relations with the Afghani Taliban and Haqqani Mujahedeen. President Musharaff was moving along well with this relationship.

Once the Russians left Afghanistan, the American government folded its operations and just left the scene. It had to pay a heavy price for this callous mistake, later on. Those very personnel of Taliban and Mujahedeen who were provided arms and ammunition by the American forces, turned against the Americans down the road.

9/11/2001 changed the world. Bin Laden and his followers staged an horrendous act against the humanity. More than three thousand innocent people of all color and race, perished in the twin towers of New York. It was a masterpiece of covert operations, no doubt about it .The whole world was shocked. President George Bush immediately took the retaliate actions; invaded Afghanistan and finished off the Taliban government within two months. In order to go to Afghanistan land locked country, Americans have to get an O.K from Pakistan. General Powell visited Pakistan and told President Musharraf in very blunt words that either cooperate with us or else. Musharraf was left with no choice except to say yes to the American General. That was the beginning of a new chapter in the U.S-Pakistan relations. Pakistan broke off the ties from Afghans Taliban officially and decided to go with the west. Some observers say that Pakistan Intelligence Agency maintained the ties covertly.

There are lot of differences between Pakistan and Afghanistan. Pakistan - economically and socially-is much stronger. It has good educational institutions, a strong governing structure and is oriented towards modern culture.

Musharraf and Pakistan army started closer ties with American military to defeat Al Qaeda and Taliban insurgents in Pakistan and Afghanistan. However, the success rate was minimal. These two militants group were entrenched along the borders of Afghanistan and Pakistan. Pakistan Mujahedeen group was also active. During this time, a political correspondent from New York Times, named Pearl was abducted from Lahore, Pakistan and was beheaded by the members of Al Qaeda and local Mujahedeen. The murderers were never caught. Two attempts were made to kill President Mushrraf, too. Pakistan was not the safe place to visit.

In 2003, U.S started the invasion of Iraq. The people of Pakistan were not happy. President Bush visited India and Pakistan in 2006.The conditions in Pakistan were so bad that President Bush had to travel in dark secrecy. There was no public contact with the President. Just few days before the arrival of the President, an American diplomat was killed by the terrorists, in Islamabad, the capital of Pakistan. Musharraf's government was not in control of the militants.

After eight years of military rule, elections were held to select the President. .In 2008, Musharraf lost the elections and Pakistan People Party (PPP) regained the control of the central government. The same year, Benazir Bhutto the most popular politician of Pakistan was killed by Taliban militants. Asif Zardari, her husband became the President of Pakistan. Nawaz Sharif, the exiled former Prime Minister returned during this democratic transition. His party-PML-N-became the opposition party, in this process. So almost after a decade, democracy was restored in Pakistan. During the last sixty years Pakistan was ruled by the military for almost thirty years.

Pakistan had become the central stage when President Nixon wanted to establish cordial diplomatic relations with Peoples Republic of China, in 1972. Pakistan had built good rapport with the Communist China, since then. Saudi Arabia and Turkey had become close friends of Pakistan; India was the arch enemy. The relations with the United States were friendly. Close cooperation from Pakistan was needed by the United States to fight a war in Afghanistan, against Al Qaeda and Taliban. Pakistan had become a strategic partner of the United States. All the military supplies had to go through the territory of Pakistan. United States was giving billions of dollars to Pakistan to fight against the Afghan Taliban and Al Qaeda militants. Bin Laden the supreme commander in chief of Al Qaeda was the mastermind behind Twin Tower tragedy in New York. It was reported that he and his group had been directing all kind of terrorist operations against America from the caves of Pak/Afghan border

UNITED STATES FOREIGN POLICY IN PAKISTAN

Going back to history, Pakistan wanted to have some kind of security from a global power, considering India as a threat. When America offered a security shield under South East Asia Treaty Organization (SEATO) Pakistan immediately joined it. President Eisenhower welcomed the Pakistan participation. In 1960, John F. Kennedy became the President; he wanted to establish close relations with India. Pakistan was standing at the side line, at that point in time. When President Bill Clinton came aboard, he was more inclined towards India rather than Pakistan. In 2005, Prime Minister of India, Dr.Man Mohan Singh, visited United States and established close relationship with President Bush. That was the turning point in the relations between India and the United States. Musharraf was the President of Pakistan at that time; he and President Bush did not hit well-personally and politically.

When Russians had invaded Afghanistan in 1979, American government wanted to move them out from the country. United States made Pakistan its strategic partner. The freedom fighters called Mujahedeen and Taliban came into existence at this juncture. I.S.I-Pakistan Intelligence Agency provided training to these people. Saudi Arabia and the United States gave the money and the arms. Russians left Afghanistan in 1989. Americans also left the scene after Russian withdrawal. These very well armed militants took up the fighting against Americans after 9/11.

Bin Laden moved to Afghanistan and Pak/Afghan border became the training ground for Al Qaeda. There are two Taliban groups-Afghan and Pakistan. The Afghan group has hard core militants and moderate recruits. The moderate Taliban members generally are from poor, religious and illiterate section of the Afghan society. The Pakistan Taliban comprises suicide bombers, and mujahedeen militants. They want to establish a government that should follow strict Sharia Laws.

Taliban and Al Qaeda organization lost the most charismatic leader in the death of Bin Laden. He was not only the figure head, master planner and money source he was like a father figure to many young recruits. The terrorist groups now consist of small independent entities; they chart out their own agenda and carry out attacks according to their planning. There is no central command; there are many splintered groups. The main objective of all of them is to create a sense of insecurity, un-stability and fear. These outfits want to inflict maximum loss of innocent lives and economic fall.

No organization can carry out its objective without the supply of ample money. United States and other western countries should impose strict rules and regulations to cut off the sources of money supply to these terrorists organizations-individually and collectively. This is the most important step in choking the operations of these criminals. In Pakistan, there are many more terrorist groups like- Let, which carried out massacre in Mumbai, India-besides Taliban and Mujahedeen. The unfortunate part in the fight against these terrorist, is that the Pakistan government is not that strong to take action against these groups. So they are thriving well and doing the killing, at will.

Pakistan is well known as one of the most corrupt nations in the world. The Present President of Pakistan, Asif Zardari was nicknamed Mr.10%.During the regime of Benazir Bhutto-his wife-he held the position of Commerce Minister; it was said that in order to get any government contract, they have to pay ten percent of the contract value to Mr.Zardari. Before Benazir Bhutto, Nawaz Sharif was the Prime-Minister and he made millions in kickback and bribes. Pakistan military generals ruled the country without knowing anybody how much money they puffed in their sacks. The corruption circle was present everywhere and the general public could do nothing.

When you are dealing with such countries like Pakistan, you have to think twice where to start in laying down your goals and objectives. The foreign policy of the United States had made erroneous mistakes in the past for supporting kings, Presidents and Prime-Ministers who were autocratic, corrupt and self centered.

Right now, the United States is focused on Al Qaeda, Taliban and other terrorists organizations-how to wipe them out, that is the main policy objective. Since Afghanistan is a land locked country, all the military supplies have to travel through Pakistan territory. This is one of the most important considerations for making Pakistan a strategic partner. The other factor is that Afghan Taliban militants are well entrenched in Pak/Afghan border area. It was a shock and a big surprise to find that Bin Laden had been living in Pakistan right near the capital of the country, Islamabad for five years and the Pakistan government never gave any inkling of it, to the U.S government. Many observers feel that Pakistan was playing a double role, all along.

As mentioned before, Al Qaeda and Taliban operatives are fighting a guerilla war and it is tough to win this kind of war. They know where to run and hide and where to stage a surprise attack. It is true that Pakistan intelligence agency has good connections with the Afghan Taliban and it has been supporting them. The policy makers in the United States must not forget that Pakistan want to play a dominant role in future Afghan government set up, once American leave the country; it does not want to see any Indian influence. When the United States is thinking of opening dialogue with moderate Afghan Taliban, it would be a smart move to take Pakistan out of the loop from this activity; Pakistan along with Taliban operatives would then run the government of Afghanistan, otherwise. It would be too late then.

The best solution for the United States would be to minimize its role in Afghanistan and let the United Nations Security Forces take up the training task of the Afghan army. The afghan government should be strong enough to take care of its defenses and security. Afghanistan would take a long time to become a normal state free from drugs and poverty.

The relations with Pakistan should be looked from many angles .Pakistan wants to be in good friendly relations with the United States mainly because it wants financial aid and military hardware. It wants to have a mediator for

Kashmir dispute with India. Pakistan has been using terrorist flag in promoting its interests. The most trust worthy friend of Pakistan is China. Russia and China are close friends, too. In any global conflict, Russia, China and Pakistan could pose a common threat against the United States and other western countries. North Korea and Iran are two other countries that could become serious trouble makers against the Americans.

There are three strategic considerations that Pakistan is keeping up its sleeves. Keeping good relations with Afghans Taliban, headed by Omar Abdullah make sense for Pakistan. In such situation, Strategy Number would be: use these militants against India; number two: with the help of Afghan Taliban, Pakistan can exert a very dominant role in Afghanistan and the third strategy is connected with the long range planning. Specifically this strategy would be to train the terrorists in Pakistan hilly regions, against the United States, India, England and other western countries.

Under these conditions, United States has to look into all ramifications of the dangers that could spring up if ignored. Pakistan would then, have the capability of launching terror attacks against its perceived enemies. And in reality, it could become the breeding ground for all kind of terrorist activities to be staged against the United States. Building Strategic partnership with Pakistan may insure that this scenario may disappear. Breaking up with Pakistan would not be a good step when we look into the seriousness of the break up. However, this relationship would require regular review from the United States foreign policy planners.

United States has been using drones-pilotless planes- to attack hiding militants especially in Waziristan, the north western part of Pakistan. In these attacks, sometime civilians are also killed. General Kayani, Pakistan Army Chief strongly criticized the Americans for using these drone attacks. In 2011, an American CIA agent killed two Pakistanis; this incident became a big issue between Pakistan and the United States. And then the most explosive event-the killing of Bin Laden by American Commandos without informing Pakistan government took place. This incident got the global attention. The questions of complicity and incompetency were raised by the Americans; Pakistan rebutted by saying that it is absurd. At present, the relations between these two countries are sitting on a very flimsy ground. President Obama and his team is looking for some acceptable and verifiable solutions to protect the interests of the United States. Some political gurus are saying that Pakistan would not change its policies of covert support to Afghan Taliban.

The United States foreign policy planners should take into stride the following important factors. Poverty and illiteracy, high unemployment, corruption and break down of legal system, a strong religious community, animosity with India and feelings of revenge, prevailing anti-American views and incompetent governing bodies. Democracy has returned to Pakistan after almost ten years but it is the military which is more powerful than the civilian government. If the economic conditions do not improve in the near future, it would not be surprising to see a bloodless coup and a military general would be sitting at the top of the government structure.

VIET NAM

The Socialist Republic of Viet Nam was established in 1976. It has a population of 90 millions; the capital cities are Hanoi and Ho Chi Minh previously known as Saigon. It is a Communist state; it is trying to follow the Chinese model of Capitalistic government. Per Capita income is roughly $1,170 with Gross Domestic Product around 102 Billions. Major export countries are U.S, E.U, Japan and China. The yearly export to the U.S is approximately 14 Billions and import figures are 3.7 Billions. The literacy figures are very high-94%; fifty percent of population is Buddhists and there are ten percent Christians.

Back in 1885, the French Imperialists had occupied Viet Nam, Cambodia and Laos and named this territory as French Indo-China. Later on, Japanese took over these countries during World War II. After the defeat of Japanese, French tried to re establish themselves but in 1954, the North Viet Nam army routed the French in the battle of Dien Bieu Phu and that was the end of the French Connection. In 1961, President Kennedy sent American military advisors and a small contingent of armed forces to South Viet Nam. That was the beginning of the American involvement in Viet Nam. President Lyndon Johnson sent more troops and finally President Nixon started a full scale war in Indo-China. However, this war proved very damaging to the U.S prestige; thousands of soldiers and civilians were killed. Finally, Viet Nam guerrilla fighters snatched their victory with resounding success; United States had to leave the country in 1975 with a defeat. It was a humiliating experience for the country.

The world never stops in moving to new directions and time erases the sad memories. Normal relations were restored with Viet Nam by President Clinton in 1995. President Bush visited Viet Nam in 2006 and lent a supporting hand to the government of Viet Nam. The new generation of Viet Nam is not anti-U.S; rather it is pro-United States. If ever there was a conflict between China and the United States, Viet Nam government would support the United States and not China. Viet Nam wants U.S investment in their country and move forward.

It is interesting to note that Dr.Ho Chi Minh-the father of Viet Nam's independent movement-and Pundit Nehru of India had established good personal relations during the time when North Viet Nam was trying to dislodge the French occupation. Indian National Congress had supported the Viet Nam's independence from the French. At the present moment, Indian relations with Viet Nam are cordial and friendly. Some Indian companies -Birla and Tata's have started investing in the country. President of India Pratibha Patil visited Viet Nam in 2011 and promised to increase the trade and other connections.

Viet Nam is emerging as a vibrant country; it needs foreign investments and it has to build a stable governing structure. No country can move forward unless there is an environment of business growth, availability of technical know how and sound government policies to encourage entrepreneurs and multi national companies. Sound business practices and abundant supply of smart work force would ultimately move the country in the right direction; it may not be as dramatic as the Chinese but it would be significant. United States should assist the Viet Nam government efforts to make it a stronger nation economically as well as militarily. It is in the interest of the United States to see it happen.

Neighbors

Russia was the next door neighbor in the sense that it helped Viet Nam economically as well militarily till 1989 when it cut off its assistance program. In fact, China was getting concerned when Russia was deeply involved in Viet Nam affairs. Viet Nam had a sizeable minority of Chinese descent but in 1979 about 500,000 people of Chinese origin –known as boat people- were forced out of the country during the border clashes with China. Historically speaking Viet Nam had fought against Chinese with courage many times before. At the present juncture, Russian influence in Viet Nam has almost disappeared. In its place, the American presence is visibly felt in all walks of life.

The most important border country is China. Because of its size, population, economic clout and military strength, Viet Nam can not ignore the fact that it can not take chances with this emerging Super Power. China knows the strength of Viet Nam; it has defeated Japanese, French and the mighty United States so there is no big deal to tackle Chinese if any thing goes wrong. The present government of Viet Nam wants to maintain a friendly foreign policy towards China but with certain reservations. It has raised its concern about the sovereignty claim of Chinese over oil and gas rich islands in South China Sea. Very recently, Viet Nam had invited India to explore the possibility of finding oil and gas in certain islands located in that region. Very promptly, China raised the opposition and warned India to keep off. Chinese government is telling other countries that it would settle this matter peacefully. United States is getting involved in this matter on behalf of other Asian countries. Let us see.

As mentioned before, India and Viet Nam had in the past established good friendly relations mainly because of the common thread of gaining independence from the colonial rule. Leaders of both countries wanted freedom for their countries and that was the starting point. The present government of India headed by Dr.Man Mohan Singh has declared publicly to follow the policy to look towards East meaning there by to pay importance to the countries of East Asia. Further to note, it is a well known fact that Viet Nam had stood the pressure of the Chinese army. In this context establishing friendship with Viet Nam, in case of any future conflict with China, India has a good reason to find a resourceful ally. At the same token, Viet Nam government knows very well the potential advantage of having India on its side. Viet Nam and India have a mutual interest to further their cooperation in trade and other related matters.

Viet Nam has a common border with Cambodia; a country of fifteen million people and famous for Hindu and Buddhist temples built around 9-12th century. Angkor Vat temples are examples of some of the very best Hindu architecture. They are located at the borders of Thailand and Cambodia. In 1975, Cambodia was over run by the Communist party called Khemer Rouge. Its leader Pot Pot wanted to set up a rural utopian society with no need for any money, rich and educated people. About two million people were killed and tortured by the Pot Pot regime between1975-79. Viet Nam intervened in this genocide in 1979 and got rid of Pot Pot murderers. Khemer Rouge had the support of Chinese Communist Party; Viet Nam army routed the rascals and established a humane government. Credit should be given to Viet Nam for destroying Pot Pot.

United States and Viet Nam
Where does Viet Nam fit into United States strategic partnership in Asia?-that's an important question to ask. We have to address this question based upon the past relationship of the country with Russia and China. Normal relations with Viet Nam were restored only ten years ago. Past hostilities have been hatched but it should not be forgotten that it takes some time before a genuine friendly environment could be established between Viet Nam and the United States. Some American companies like Intel and others have set up manufacturing facilities in Viet Nam and are helping the country in different other areas. The Russian assistance-economic as well as military-has almost disappeared. After the boat episode in 1979 when 500,000 people of Chinese origin were expelled by Viet Nam, the Chinese government would be reluctant to extend any helping .hand to Viet Nam. This is an important factor that United States policy makers should take into consideration while laying out long term policies for Viet Nam.

Viet Nam needs foreign investment besides other kind of assistance in Education, Health Care, Military training and infra structure. United States, Japan, South Korea and possibly India are the only countries that could provide some help in these areas. Among other countries, United States has the highest stake in this collaboration with Viet Nam. It will take few decades for Viet Nam to come to the level of South Korea in terms of economic and military strength; so it will be a slow and gradual process for the United States to provide substantial aid to Viet Nam. United States would like to have an ally like South Korea to build a solid base against a potential Super Power China; Viet Nam could prove to be a reliable friend.

Following the same analogy, India would like to build stronger relations with Viet Nam. China and India are bound to face each other in the coming near future in East and South Asia. China has already a well rounded ally in Pakistan which would be ready to go against India any time whenever that situation arises. On record, India and Pakistan have already waged two wars between them. Kashmir is still a hot issue; China would back up Pakistan.

The ever present thorny and complex problem of Taiwan is not going to go away soon. United States needs as many friends as possible to stand up against China; Japan, Australia, Philippines and South Korea would line up with the

United States; Viet Nam and possibly India might also back up the United States if the worse scenario shows up its face. However, there are pretty good chances that China may never take a bold step to attack Taiwan and that would save the world from a big catastrophe. In the global political scene, major confrontations between great powers are having lesser and lesser chances to come alive. Iran and North Korea are the exceptions. Dictators do not care for humanity and common man; they could unleash a senseless war according to their whim and ego. These two countries of Asia are going to give headache not only to the United States but they could cause world wide upheaval and misery.

If Viet Nam runs into any serious confrontation with any country, there are good indications that it might ask for United States help. So it is in the common interest of the Viet Nam and United States to forge a stronger alliance between them and that would prove advantageous to both countries in the long run.

BURMA

Burma also known now as Myanmar got its independence from Britain in 1948. The civilian rule lasted for about a decade and from 1962 to 2011, military Junta ruled the country and converted it as one of the poorest nations of Asia. The international community could do nothing against the military rulers. It became a country where all the power rested with the ruling military Junta. In 1989 national elections were held and Aung San Suu Kyi, daughter of Independence hero Aung San won the elections. However, the military rulers put her behind the bars for fifteen years. The whole world had condemned the actions of the military rulers. United Nations sent its envoy to Rangoon to get release of Suu Kyi from her house arrest and then in 2011, the military Junta, once again held the elections and at this time ,Aung San Suu Kyi got her independence. It was a pleasant gift to the democratic set up for the country. Finally, Myanmar, it seemed was on its way to a brighter future.

Secretary of State Hillary Clinton flew to Rangoon and met with Aung San Suu Kyi; she also announced that United States would remove Sanctions which were imposed during the military rule. Not only the United States, but United Kingdom and European Union along with other nations welcomed the change in Burma and promised to provide all kinds of assistance to the new political structure. It was hoped that the military Junta would let the civilian governing body to perform its duties and let the democracy thrive again.

The present political structure in the country is just a beginning; it has to be watched closely how things turn out in the future. Will the military Junta come back again after letting the democratic process to establish itself for a short period of time; it is a big question mark. Aung San Suu Kyi is well known in Burma and in the world but after she is gone or displaced by the Junta for any excuse, the military establishment would have a valid reason to reestablish its bases in the country. Looking from that point of view, Burma would go back to dictatorship and anarchy. It would be unfortunate but it could happen.

In the whole world, China was the only country to support the military junta of Myanmar. The Indian government had also started leaning in that direction. However, when the changes started taking place in the country, the entire world moved towards Aung San Suu Kyi. Let us hope that the military junta let the democratic process establish itself on a firm footing. Pakistan is one example where the military kept on changing the rules of the game and thus entrenched itself again and again. It is up to the leaders of the Burmese people to assert themselves and throw out the shackle of military rule once for all.

Since Burma is just emerging from military rule, it would be a far sighted thinking to lay the foundation of strong friendly ties with the United States. Right now, China is the only country that has been providing financial support to the ruling military junta. United States is in a position to come up with a solid economic, military and technical assistance package. It may take sometime to recoup the lost ground but it would be worthwhile to regain the confidence of the Burmese leaders and the general public as such. The enlightened leadership of Burma would be willing to grab a generous offer from the United States. By following this policy of genuine help, United States might very well line up a solid ally. The foreign policy of the United States should be fashioned in such a way that it keeps up listing up more and more friends around the globe It is very clear that China would like to exert its influence over South East Asia and losing Burma to Chinese area of influence would be a mistake.

It is true that the investment made now in the Burmese economy would be based upon long term returns. Presently the country does not have a large standing army nor does it have modern military equipment. From that point of view United States should entertain the idea of starting a joint military co-operation. This long term planning would require regular watch and necessary adjustments because the situation is still very fluid and unpredictable.

The present President of Burma-a military general-is not making any kind of commitment that the military would allow full fledged democracy in the country; he however, is also not saying no to the aid programs being offered by many countries. England, Japan, India, European Union and others have indicated their willingness to help the Burmese government in terms of investment, training and other kinds of assistance. It seems likely that the Burmese government would accept these offers and would not go for any specific collaboration with any one county. That means that United States may not become an exclusive partner of progress and forward momentum.

We must remember that Burma was one of the founding nations of the Non Aligned Movement along with India, China and Indonesia. There is a very good probability that Burma might once again join the Non Aligned Campus. Just like India, it may lean towards United States but at the same time never commit itself to one country. One thing is sure it will not fall under the influence of Russia. Buddhism and Communism do not go together. India and China might become close partners of the emerging Burma because of the past historical connections.

Where Burma goes from here, has a crucial outcome for the rest of the countries of Asia. The western countries especially the United States and other Asian countries of South and South East Asia should make all efforts to see Aung San Suu Kyi succeed in her journey to make Burma a democratic country. Look at the scenario when she is not able to deliver the promise land to the Burmese people;that will be chaotic .The democratic structure would fall down by its own undoing and failure. It would mean an open invitation to the military ybosses to take up the reign of the government once again .That would be tragic.

BANGLADESH

Bangladesh got its independence from Pakistan after a bitter battle in 1971.Indias Prime Minister Mrs Indra Gandhi was instrumental in creating a new country of Bangladesh. Richard Nixon and Henry Kissinger were furious at India's support to the freedom fighters of Bangladesh; it was too late and Pakistan forces faced a crushing defeat. Millions of Bangladeshi citizens were butchered by the Pakistani armed forces in this fight for freedom.

Bangladesh is a small country and a poor country with lot of problems. Illiteracy, unemployment, corruption and personal grudges among the politicians have taken a heavy toll on the economical front of the country. The only country that has shown keen interest in developing the overall well being of the Bengali citizens is India. Very recently, India's Prime-Minister Dr.Singh offered a line of credit of one billion dollars to the Bengali government to implement infra structure projects. Sheikh Hasina, the daughter of the founder of Bangladesh Sheik Mujeebur Rehman, is the current Prime-Minister of Bangladesh. She has established good relations with Sonia Gandhi, President of Indian Congress Party and other Indian leaders. And that is a good beginning.

In the arena of International diplomacy, self interest of the country carries a big weight. As a global power, United States policy framers have to see where the resources have to be spent. For a country which does not have a sizeable military, does not possess any economic clout and is ravaged with all kinds of uncertainty, Bangladesh does not attract keen interest from the United States. In 2012, Secretary of State Hillary Clinton paid a visit to Bangladesh but did not spell out any assistance program for the country. Prime Minister Sheik Hasina must be disappointed with the visit.

Looking from a broad perspective, it could be concluded that right now Bangladesh is in bad shape but down the road it might become a good and attractive place to invest in its future. United States has to start from the scratch in terms of economic aid, technical assistance and military help and keep up building the structure. It might take a few years to build that friendly gesture towards Bangladesh and its people but if it is done on a genuine basis, there are pretty good chances that Bangladesh would become a reliable partner of the United States. The plus side of Bangladesh is that it is not infected with terrorist organizations and it is looking for partners who could make a positive change in their country. Just after Bangladesh became independent Senator Kennedy did go to Bangladesh and indicated that United States would be sympathetic towards the country; however, nothing concrete materialized in that direction.

Like India and Burma, Bangladesh might choose to go towards Non Aligned path. In such a case, European Union, England, Japan and the United States would hesitate to put their money into Bangladesh's economy. This will ultimately delay the process of industrialization, modernization and economic progress. It is the dynamism of the country's leadership that makes it or break it. Leaders of Bangladesh have to create a climate of stability and confidence for foreign investors to invest in its economy. Personal charm and common goals and objectives between leaders of two countries could really make a big difference in creating an environment of faith and goodwill. Bangladesh needs this quality in its leaders to forge such connections between United States, England, European Union, Japan, India and other countries and itself.

When we look at various countries of Asia, we find that it is the leadership quality of the country that decides who goes forward and who remains in the status quo mode or even go down the hill. Corruption, lack of administrative skills, business knowledge and a will to succeed in making the country go forward are important factors that shape the destinies of the countries. Foreign investor looks for a flourishing business environment and ease of conducting business. Infrastructure, educated work force, stability and promise of a brighter future, government support and rule of law-all of these factors entice the internal as well as external job creators. It does take time for countries which are just emerging from foreign rule. Bangladesh right now is in this position and it is no wonder that it would be sometime in the future that it attained that position. Till then, progress would be slow.

At one point in time, China, India and South Korea were at this cross road and look now where they are placed now. We can compare other countries like Pakistan and Afghanistan with the prize winners and see what made them go astray in persuing their national goals.

Looking from this context, United States should draw up a long range planning for Bangladesh. We can expect some good results only in the long term basis because Bangladesh is not there to take off because of so many shortcomings in the present system. But it would be a mistake to ignore the country because of its non compliance of basic criteria .How a country would change with the change in time, under different circumstances is difficult to predict. It is though reasonably correct to assume that Bangladesh is a safer bet than Afghanistan or Pakistan because of religious bigotry and violence prevailing in those countries .Bangladesh is a Muslim country and like Indonesia people are tolerant of other religions. That is a plus side. Bangladeshi citizens also know it very well that it was Hindu India that created their country and they should be thankful for it.

Right now Bangladesh is not looking towards China or Russia for any kind of help. In the long term process it will surely lean towards England and the United States to remove poverty, illiteracy and all other non progressive elements.

Taking clue from the Indian foreign policy testaments of "Looking East", it can be said with good predictions that India would be a good source of investment in Bangladesh economy and they would become good allies. India and Bangladesh has many things in common; the greatest common factor is the Bengali language. Ravindernath Tagore, the Noble Prize winner for literature is as much respected in Bangladesh as he is in India.

Summarizing the needs and objectives for the United States foreign policy towards Bangladesh, it could be summed up by saying that this country has the potentials of becoming a good friend and ally of the United States .It may take some time but it is worth the efforts. It may be a zigzag roadmap but it has a clear destination.

SRI LANKA

Ceylon now called Sri Lanka is a beautiful island located at the southernmost tip of India. It was beset with violence and upheaval for the last two decades or so. A military clash was going on between minority Tamil citizens and majority Sinhalese; finally in 2009 it was over. The Tamil Tigers were defeated and Mahinder Rajapaksa was reelected as President of Sri Lanka.

The battle that was going on between Tamils and Sinhalese was based upon a master plan to create a new state exclusively for Tamils. Indian government had provided all the support to Sri Lanka to suppress this so called independence movement started by Tamil Tigers, an organization similar to Irish Republic Army of Ireland. The Indian Prime-Minister Rajiv Gandhi was assassinated by the members of the Tamil Tigers for supporting Sri Lanka government.

It has been alleged that thousand of civilian Tamils were murdered by the Sri Lankan army to eliminate the Tamil Tigers members. A United Nation Commission is now looking into this matter. Since Tamil people came from India originally, the Indian government does want a fair and equitable settlement for the Tamil population.

A country of twenty million people, Sri Lanka has a Gross National Income of $ 2,200 per capita (2010). Tourism, Textiles, Tea and gems are the main sources of revenue. Buddhism, Hinduism and Christianity are the major religions of the country.

After twenty five years of civil war, Sri Lanka is recovering from stagnation and non progression .The government now has started focusing on national growth and reconstruction. This is the time when friendly nations should come to aid the government efforts. European Union and other nations had withdrawn the preferential treatment to the goods exported from Sri Lanka because of allegations of human rights violation against the civilian Tamil population. It will take some time when Sinhalese and Tamils would reconcile their political differences and start building confidence between them. Rehabilitation and settlement of displaced Tamil families along with financial assistance would go a long way to start a new chapter in the country's troubled history.

Sri Lanka is a member state of Commonwealth nations and there is no dictatorship or military supremacy; democracy is thriving well and good. However, the wounds of long term animosity and anger between Tamils and Sinhalese would take some time to heal. Sinhalese have to give full respect to their minority Tamil citizens in order to bring progress and prosperity to the nation. Countries like India, England and United States can play a major role in uplifting the country from its present not too happy situation. It will be a case of mutual benefits for all.

We have to examine now what role United States should play at this junction of Sri Lankan history? As a Super power, United States has to look from long term as well as short term policy planning. Because of the existing conflict in the country, foreign nations were reluctant to enter into Sri Lankan territory. But this situation has changed now and it is very appropriate to take the first step towards this goal. The sooner these steps are taken, better would be the results. The time is ripe now to extend all kinds of support to the Sri Lankan government in its quest to develop their country. It is presumed that there would be peace and stability in the country otherwise no country would put its stake in Sri Lanka. Another important factor that has to be recognized is that the leaders of the country should not carry the baggage of corruption in their hands; otherwise it would be waste of time and waste of scare resources.

Building a nation is not an easy task; it is so essential to have the requisites institutions to build a firm structure of a modern thriving nation. Educated workforce, peace and stability, rule of law, favorable government rules and regulations, natural resources, efficient infrastructure, transparency of government administration, non corrupt leadership at federal and provincial levels, incentives for local and foreign investors-these and other related factors have to be in their places to make things happen. Some countries take a long time to put these factors in their right places and a few do it with ease and efficiency and in a shorter span of time. It all depends upon the will and dedication of the people and their leaders. Countries like South Korea and Taiwan are shining examples of successful transformations .The question is where Sri Lanka stands today considering the above mentioned requirements. The answer to that question is: it will take a long time for it to come near the required level, After twenty five years of constant fighting, the country has to reestablish a reasonable governing structure. Countries who are interested in helping Sri Lanka must take a long view of everything. It applies to United States too. Short term objectives may be the starting points.

At present United States does not have a concrete plan to assist Sri Lanka; it is true that United States has to evaluate thoroughly its investment strategies. Every country is different and political conditions keep on changing on a constant basis. So it is not an easy task to write down foreign policy note book. United States stands for propagating democracy in other countries; it stands for freedom of speech and individual freedom besides other well defined declarations. Sri Lanka does meet those basic principles. What it needs is help in setting up good educational institutions, help in raising agricultural output, building health clinics in rural areas and similar other activities. United States has a vast reservoir of technically trained personnel who could really make a difference in uplifting the standard of living of the common man and woman of Sri Lanka. Step by step, the assistance program should be upgraded to meet the growing needs of the country.

It may be noted down that Sri Lanka has shown no desire to accept Chinese help in reconstructing its economy. The relations between the two countries are cordial but nothing more than that. China has not extended any assistance package to Sri Lanka. This very factor should make the foreign policy makers of the United States to think what it means and how best this situation should be utilized for the benefit of the United States global interests. Sri Lanka did belong to the non aligned group. To change this position, something must be done by the United States. It is a good opportunity for United States to invest in Sri Lanka whole heartedly. It is going to bring good results for both countries..

TAIWAN

In 1949, Mao's forces made KMT (Nationalist Party) commander in chief General Chiang to flee to the island of Taiwan. Ever since Communist China is proclaiming to the world that Taiwan is an integral part of China. However, Republic of China (Taiwan) has been an independent country since 1950. After many twists and turns, United States has acknowledged that China has special connections with Taiwan. It was pointed out that Taiwan and Communist China have to work out a peaceful and sustainable solution. In the mean time a special document was signed by Taiwan and the United States to guarantee the freedom of Taiwan in case it is attacked by mainland China. In other words United States would be obliged to defend Taiwan against Chinese aggression if and when that happens. China has kept the pressure on Taiwan but nothing has happened.

In a short span of time, Taiwan has achieved outstanding progress; starting from a poor agricultural economy, it has transformed itself as a roaring giant. The Gross Domestic Product based upon Purchasing Power Parity is\$ 885 billions; the present rate of growth is 6.5%. Gross National Income Index is \$32k. Unemployment is low at 4% , people living below poverty level is only 1.1%- an impressive figure. Taiwan is facing shortage of young people because the average birth rate is one child per family. The present population (2011) is 23millions. It has gained number four position in terms of foreign reserve holdings just behind Japan, China and Russia. All these four countries are export oriented economies and have established themselves as outstanding global exporters. Taiwan exports Electronic goods, Plastic making equipment, Textiles and Petro chemical products. It can boast of having the second tallest building in the world. Buddhism, Taoism and Christianity are flourishing in the land.

Till 2000 KMT politicians ruled over the island but then Progressive Democratic Party defeated the Nationalists in the election and Party Leader Chen Shui-bian became the President. He announced his intentions to make Taiwan an independent country. Communist China was furious and threatened to take military action. Short range missiles were placed in active positions. That made President Chen little bit nervous; he immediately approached United States and made huge amount of purchases of military equipment including Skud missiles and advanced warning radar systems. Beijing got the message and nothing happened. However, it was the time of tension and unpredictable consequence. As time passed, normal conditions were restored.

When we look at the leadership quality of the global powers, we can make some kind of vague but reliable assessment of their thinking in terms of starting a deadly war. It is no secret that Wars do not solve the problems; they only aggravate the situation. Only immature dictators and leaders would indulge in starting a war because it results in huge waste of resources and undesirable loss of human lives. Discussion and exchange of various agendas have become a more desirable media of resolving conflicts. Judging from this point of view, it is very unlikely that China would take military action against Taiwan .

CONCLUSION

Every day something new happens in this world that changes the dynamics of our thinking. World War II changed the status of the United States. The beginning of the twenty first century heralded new world powers into picture. Russia receded from Super Power platform. United States of America took up the most prestigious award as the most powerful country in the world.

For few decades there were no challenges to the supremacy of the United States but that is not the case now. The socio-economic transformation in the world has brought forward China as the most up coming world power. No single European power can match the potentials of emerging Asian countries.

The game of world politics would be played by countries like Brazil, China, India, Russia and the United States, in the coming decades. Like in any situation, safeguards, threats and possibilities have to be evaluated on a regular basis to keep the position safe and sound. United States of America has a full field to fill in its world wide foreign policy planning. Our study has spanned on East and South East Asian countries; it does not cover the Middle East.

The most important question that has to be addressed is: How the United States is going to keep its present position as the Supreme Power in the world specifically, its strategic position in Asia? In order to lay out any plan of actions to address this question, we have to line up the staunchest allies and potential enemies and those who fall in between the two groups. We have to go country by country. The past and the future indications could help us chart out these three categories. Let us list these countries:

Solid Allies:

Japan: Australia: South Korea: Philippines

Allies:

Thailand: India: Indonesia

Potential Threats

China: North Korea: Iran

Middle Group

Pakistan: Afghanistan: Malaysia

We shall start with those countries which fall under the category of Solid Allies. If we analyze the global political arena, all these four countries have supported the position of the United States for the last twenty years or more. These countries could be counted by the United States as genuine all weather friends. Off and on there could be some differences of opinion on different subject matters among these countries, but at the end of the day they will be in sync. South Korea for sure would like to have American troops in their land because of unpredictable dictatorship in North Korea. Japan too, would like to have the safety umbrella from the American military whether they would be posted in Okinawa or some where else. Australia would not jeopardize its independence from the Chinese threats. It could be possible only when United States have its sway in the region.

Friendly but Independent Allies: India, Indonesia and Thailand belong to this category. The present trend of Indian and Indonesian leadership is to lean towards United States; but they could not be taken for granted. We feel it is sixty forty relationship matrix. Both of these countries under the leaderships of Nehru and Sukarno were neutral to anti U.S. The Russian influence was much deeper in India and Indonesia. That was not the case in Thailand. Communism in Thailand was out of question. As we know Thailand had been the only Asian country that never came under any European domination. Monarchy, Military and Buddhism have ruled Thailand. U.S-Thailand relations have maintained cordial and friendly interactions between them for a long period of time. However, in the recent past, Thailand has been leaning towards China .Prime-Minister Thaksin Shinawatra had been showing keen interest in taking Thai-China relations to higher grounds.

India and Indonesia have started realizing the powerful influence of emerging China, in that part of the world. United States has taken a big foreign policy turn under President Bush to bring India into its orbit. Prime-Minister Man Mohan Singh of India too, feels that United States and India could really become close friends. Secretary of State Hillary Clinton while on a state visit to India made a statement that India should take up the leadership role in Asia; implying that it should challenge China in that capacity. Indian leadership may not completely embrace American friendship and might like to follow an independent policy to some extent. That scenario holds good in case of Indonesia.

Dynamics of global politics always present some thorny issues to be resolved delicately and imaginatively. To bring India, Indonesia and Thailand into American Influence and count them as solid allies would require patient and careful handling on the part of top U.S leaders and officials.

Potential Threats: China with the title of the second largest economy in the world is the biggest threat to the United States Supremacy in the Asian region. North Korea and Iran come next in line. These three countries can cause upheavals in the Asian continent. No Asian country including India can affectively challenge their potentially dangerous manipulations. None of these countries are democracies in the true sense of the world and are governed by dictators of some kind .China and North Korea are bound with military treaties; Iran stand alone. At one point in history, the Shah of Iran was one of the most reliable friends of the United States and today, the President of Iran is the deadliest foe of America. China has a mature leadership but North Korea and Iran have revolutionary leaders who can do anything whatever they think is right. These kinds of people are like Hitler; the world would be better off without them. Iran and North Korea could trigger a mini war in the Asian peninsula against South Korea or Israel.

It is difficult to predict what would be the best way to handle Iranian and North Korean situation. Co-operation with Russia and China is essential to solve this knotty and dangerous problem. United States alone may not be able to handle this serious situation. South Korea's Sun Shine policy may work out with

North Korea. At the same token, Russia's influence in the Middle East may eradicate or at least lessen the Iranian threat.

Middle Group: Malaysia is the most suitable candidate to embrace American friendship in this group; unlike the old anti-U.S rhetoric, the present Malaysian leadership is open for friendly U.S dialogue. Like Indonesia, it is a moderate Muslim country. It is a country where Muslim militants have not found popular support in the general public. By Asian standard, it is a well to do country. A complete turn around in mutual relationship may not be possible in the near future; however, a gradual process of improved relationship may very well be a good possibility. American foreign policy should be geared to this objective.

Afghanistan: It is a country where British failed and where the Russians quit in defeat. All the money and military resources of the United States and other countries to finish off Taliban and Al Quaeda elements would not be a success. It is unfortunate but a truth that Afghan society is still very primitive in this modern age; tribalism and old age customs and traditions still prevail amongst the majority of people. All the money and military force of the western countries would not make any big dent in this environment. History tells us that society changes gradually-most of the time-and drastic steps do not bring about desired results. It will be sheer wastage of money and human lives to drastically change Afghanistan. American government should make a truce with the Taliban and put pressure on them that they would not violate human rights and would not follow decadent rules and laws which discriminate against the women. President Obama's policy in Afghanistan is on the right track. Let Afghan people decide the pace of change in government, social and economic reforms; the outsiders may not succeed in this transformation process.

Pakistan: It is not a failed state but it might shift in that direction fast if the leaders of the country do not change their corrupt practices. Billions of American dollars could not bring down Haqqani militants; local Taliban and other extremist groups have the courage and freedom to bring the government to its knees. The military generals are the real rulers of the country; no body can predict when the military would just take over from the civilian government. In the past sixty years, they ruled the country for almost thirty years. Pakistan military would not venture to take action against Balouchi and Pathan militants who are the de facto rulers of the Afghan-Pakistan border. The American pressure on Pakistan military to wage war against these freedom fighters would not materialize. The Pak government would take the money from the United States and tell that they are doing every thing that is possible but in reality they would do nothing. This money would go waste as far as the U.S objectives are concerned. Majority of Pakistani people do not like Americans. American policy makers should make a note of it while laying down their plan of actions. Pakistan might return to normal conditions when there would be no action against the militants. It is true Pakistan eventually would turn corners and become a safe and stable country but it may not happen in the near future.

The situation in Pakistan is serious and dangerous. It is a nuclear state and militants might like to take advantage of the weakness of the Pakistan government. United States and other countries should be aware of this situation.

U.S Foreign Policy across Asia: Every new event calls for new direction; however, the basic structural objectives remain in tact. Safety and Security of the country is the governing factor in laying out specific action plans; Monetary Advantage comes next. In other words, Safety and Prosperity of the country propel the foreign policy.

When a country is sitting at the top of the tracking board, many considerations have to be accommodated in proper places. As the sole Super Power in the world, United States has to chart its foreign policy in a unique and exclusive manner. Past interactions with different countries and future projections of the global events help in drawing detailed plans. Wrong information and faulty conclusions could lead to terrible end results. President Bush decision to invade Iraq is the glaring example of this scenario.

The policy planners have to figure out who are the solid allies, which countries are potential foes and who are in between. Based upon this information, customized foreign policy packages should be prepared for each country. The policy should address three areas namely: (a) keep the existing allies in tact (b) bring the independent group into your orbit (c) prepare different plan of actions to fight the enemies. If these areas are covered with maturity and accuracy, the results would speak for them in the future.

Spanning the recent developments in North Africa and Middle East, some revolutionary events have taken place. The Arab Spring has risen in the horizon. Starting from Tunisia, Egypt, Yemen and Libya, dictators have been thrown out and democracy is taking roots. It is too early to predict what direction this movement will take shape. The whole world is noticing these changes and countries are adjusting their policies to that affect. United States, as the most vocal advocate of democracy, has to play a big role in all these dramatic changes. These countries need some guidance and assistance in transforming these remarkable changes into history making events.

The troubling locations in Asia are North Korea, Pakistan, Afghanistan, Iran and Palestine. The core Power Block consisting Russia, China, North Korea, Iran and Pakistan could face the other Block, in case of any unforeseen crisis. This Block contains Australia, Japan, South Korea, Philippines and Israel. India, Indonesia and Malaysia-three independent Middle Group countries-have the potentials of becoming pro-U.S. Tactical diplomacy and genuine fraternity interactions with these countries would pay good dividends to the United States.

In the next few decades, China would challenge the supremacy of the United States in Pacific and South East Asia. United States can maintain its status as the sole Super Power provided it is economically sound and strong in terms of military strength. China has to play lot of catch up game. Russia in the mean time would be comparatively strong economically and it might like to take the Super Power seat. China would not venture to challenge the United States on Taiwan issue. However, United States might get involved in South China gas and oil rich islands. Viet Nam, Malaysia, Philippines, Japan and Korea would not let China to grab these islands without some confrontation. We hope that this situation would not take an ugly turn and start a mini war in the region. Planning for the Foreign policy of a Super Power is not an easy task. It has to be flexible.

It is well said our present world is no one's world; there are many centers of gravitation. After World War II, we were dealing with two powers-United States and Russia. It is not valid ant more; there are multiple global powers. Speaking about existing conditions in Asia, there are two regional powers: China and India. In addition, there are two external powers: United States and Russia. We can analyze and determine how much influence each of these four countries has on other Asian countries.

We are presuming that United States would not be displaced by China or any other country for few more decades as the sole Super Power. However, signs have started appearing with clarity that United Stated would have limited influence on many Asian countries as time passes by. Countries like South Korea, Australia, Philippines and Japan would be solid allies but it would have limited influence in Pakistan, Afghanistan, Laos, Cambodia, Viet Nam and Burma and certainly no influence in North Korea, Iran and China.

India, Indonesia, Malaysia, Sri Lanka, Bangladesh may be following more or less independent paths. Here, in this region, it would be India that might be exerting more influence than any other country.

Russia at this point in time has no influence in South and East Asian countries except China and North Korea. It is no doubt that China and Russia would be solid buddies in international political arena. Viet Nam and Cambodia might also keep strong ties with Russia.

Japan is a strong Economical power in Asia; however, it has no military clout. Taiwan, China, South Korea, Indonesia and Australia are the leading trading partners of Japan besides United States and European Union. It is a great resource for financial assistance for Asian countries just as Germany is for European countries.

The geopolitical scenario of the present world presents a complex mixture of multiple global powers. The foreign policy strategists have to take this view into consideration when they lay down the ground rules. More than two world powers may have crucial influence on a country depending upon the needs and national interests of that particular country. No single global power would have the monopoly of its hold on the other country.

We can vision four leading global powers namely United States and its allies, China and Russian bloc, India and its friends, Iran and North Korean Axis, operating in Asian sub continent. It may be possible that Iran and North Korea may finally disappear from the global scene.

There are strong indications that our generation and the next generation may be spared from a deadly and wasteful occurrence of horror filled World War III. Leaders of all nations now believe in debates and discussions rather than in guns and ammunitions. We have to applaud these thoughts and let the mankind live a happy and prosperous saga full of joyous events. We have to say "Bravo brave world" Let our generation build a fortress of strength and solid cooperation among all the nations of the world. United States, Russia, China, India, Brazil, Japan ,Germany and France and all the other countries can live in peace and move forward towards a more glorious future.

CRISIS IN MIDDLE EAST

The events in the Middle East have changed the direction of history in terms of social, economical and political ramifications for the people living in that region. Dictators have been thrown out and democracy is finding popular support. It all started in the Spring of 2010 and has been named the Arab Spring. Tunisia was the first country and then it spread to Libya, Egypt and finally to Syria where a civil war is going on. The most dramatic change that has taken place is that the common man and woman are not afraid to rise against the entrenched establishment any more. President Mubark of Egypt and Colonel Kadafi of Libya were eliminated with disgrace. Rebels in Syria are predicting that President Assad will also meet the same fate, sooner or later. However, Jordan and Saudi Arabia have not gone through this upheaval.

What does it mean to the rest of the world? A lot could be said in answering this question. It is true all these changes are not going to show immediate results in the lives of the people living in that part of the world. It would be a gradual process and at times painful and difficult to embrace it. In the long run, these democratic changes are bound to produce good results for the people of Africa, Middle East and for all of us. Strong dictatorial regimes, sometime brings about rapid progress for the country and democratic structure of governance fails to come up to that level of accomplishment-there is no doubt about it. Revolutions in the past have produced some outstanding changes in the society provided they had kept the momentum in the right direction. This has to be watched carefully in the Arab world.

When we talk about Middle East countries of Asia, we are talking about Iran, Iraq, Syria, Jordan, Palestine, Saudi Arabia, Kuwait, Lebanon and Yemen; Arab countries from Africa consist of Morocco, Tunisia, Algeria , Libya and Egypt. Kuwait and Lebanon did not go through general public uprising against their governments. All of these countries are Muslim countries but fortunately they are not heavily infested with terrorist organizations except Yemen and Palestine. It seems that majority of Muslim countries that include Afghanistan and Pakistan, are facing some kind of turmoil and dissatisfaction among the people.

How the government of the United States should deal with these countries, is a very crucial question. In our study we have classified Iran as an adversary nation, Afghanistan and Pakistan as unstable. It would be futile to make any kind of projection for Egypt, Tunisia, Libya and Syria. The political situation in these countries is very uncertain. None of these countries are friendly to the United States, at present. Only with the passage of time, it would be clear what kind of foreign policy would be advantageous for the United States. It is a matter of wait and see scenario.

From a traditional point of view, Saudi Arabia and Jordan are rather friendly towards the western countries and to the United States. They do not support terrorism in their countries and oppose the views of Muslim radicals. This is a good sign because United States does need the support of the Muslim countries.

SOME TROUBLE SPOTS

Starting from nowhere, China has become a Megastar with the honor of second largest economy of the world. It is growing by leaps and bound and may be it might overtake the United States in few decades. It is gratifying that China is not following the footsteps of Imperialist Japan and it is not going to threaten other neighboring countries. It is hoped so, but who knows? Oil and potentially rich in natural gas islands of South China Sea as well as Tibet's autonomous status question are pointing arrows in other directions. Japan, Viet Nam and Philippines are claiming the right of access to these islands whereas China says it falls under Chinese territory. A kind of mini war of words is going on; it seems likely that this issue would be settled amicably between China and other contending countries and any kind of trouble would be avoided.

Where does the United States stand on these issues of islands and Tibet's independence? It has been reported that it favors Japanese position on islands; furthermore, Japan is willing to buy these islands. As far as Tibetan's freedom question is concerned, United States is not showing any strong leaning towards Dalai's Lama. There is some moral support but nothing more than that. Other western countries have not taken any positive steps, either. India is not willing to take Chinese wrath after it was humiliated in 1962. It is unfortunate that Chinese are treating Tibet the same way as Japan did to China in 1937- a brutal suppression of Tibetan's culture and way of life is undergoing under the present regime of Communist China. The world is watching but nobody is courageous enough to raise a finger against the totalitarian and ruthless dictatorship. In other words the community of nations does not care for helpless Tibetan's people.

Kashmir is another spot where trouble has been brewing for the last sixty years or so. Two wars were fought between India and Pakistan on the thorny issue of territorial integration. United States is in the middle of this mess up. As a friend of India as well as a strategic and uneasy ally of Pakistan, it has not taken a very firm and uncompromising stand. Past Presidents have held different positions. Presently, President Obama feels that United States should not meddle in this issue and it is up to India and Pakistan to arrive at a mutually agreeable solution. Judging from a very sentimental and emotional point of view -India's as well as of Pakistan's –it is the best solution for all the three nations.

Countries of central Asia like Kazakastan, Uzbekistan etc are now part of Russian Commonwealth nations; they are independent but are very much under the influence of Russia. Some of these countries have started up building relations with United States. It should however be remembered that these countries could never be strong allies of the United States. There are lot of common threads between Russia and these countries-in terms of business dealings, cultural, and political structure. As a global power, United States has a stake of some sort in most of the countries of Asia and Europe. As such, it can not ignore what is happening in these countries .However, no major conflict is foreseen at this point in time. Problems would be resolved through negotiations

.

CORNERSTONES OF U.S FOREIGN POLICY

There are four major strategic considerations that shape the foreign policy of the United States. They are: (a) Maintain the Super Power Status (b) Establish friendly relations with another Super Power (c) Safe guarding non-proliferation of nuclear arms and equipment (d) Propagating and spreading the American Values. Let us review in details how these four pillars are being supported in the present world structure.

Maintain Super Power Status: When U.S.S.R collapsed in 1991, there was no nation except the United States to take up the prestigious position of Sole Super Power in the world. The next two decades held the U.S flag flying high. However, signs had started showing up challenging the U.S position; China, India and Brazil were in the race. With a fifteen trillion dollars economy and the greatest military might, no nation is close to challenge the United States, at this juncture in history. The near future is still in safe hands but the next few decades may say something else. China's economy is growing by leaps and bound and its military position is getting stronger by the day. The Chinese government is following a very aggressive policy of expansion in all the fields of global domination and influence. India, Brazil and Russia may not be able to compete against China because of major structural deficiencies. These countries would be important global players in the international arena but getting to the top position would be difficult for them.

In the context of holding the top position in the world, United States has to have substantial continuous growth in its economy which would consolidate its position to remain as number one in military terms. When this does not happen, things would start drifting in other directions. Foreign policies have close connection with the economical, social and cultural environments of that country. If these elements are weak, they would not be accepted by others. It is imperative for the United States as a nation to keep its economy healthy and robust, only then it can continue to play the role of a Super Power otherwise some body else would take its place as the time drifts by.

Establish friendly relations with another Super Power: It is a matter of time when China would threaten the supremacy of the United States. It is a similar situation when Japan had challenged the United States. United States has two options (a) Make friendly relations with the other Super Power (b) Keep an hostile attitude and show to the other Super Power that United States is still the Supreme Power; this posturing, no doubt, will evoke resentment and antagonism from the other side. United States can ask for help from western countries and at the same token, China would be inclined to take help from Russia. These two sides can start a Cold War and plunge the world in regression and uncertain future. The word of wisdom tells us that it is the peace and harmony and not animosity and bickering among the nations that would take our planet towards prosperity and happiness. The choice is ours. As and when this situation arises, it would be in the interest of both Super Powers to forge friendship and fairplay.

Non Proliferation of Nuclear Arms: There are two countries who are trying desperately to become Nuclear Powers. They are Iran and North Korea. India, Pakistan, China, Great Britain, France, Russia, Israel and United States are members of the so called Nuclear Club. As per Non-Proliferation Treaty, no country is allowed to test or manufacture nuclear arms or equipment, any more. India and Pakistan have not signed this treaty; Iran and North Korea are going full speed to become nuclear powers in defiance of world opinion. Sanctions against Iran and North Korea have not produced any tangible results so far. It has been reported many times that Israel would not let Iran become a nuclear power and it will take military action to destroy Iranian nuclear facilities. This action from Israelis would prompt massive protests from the Muslim world, without any doubt. United States would be held responsible for this action because United States is a strong ally of Israel. Muslim terrorists and militants would,, in revenge, take strong actions against the United States as well as against the western countries. This scenario is certainly not good for the peace and stability of the entire world. The question is : Can it be avoided? Yes, it can be avoided if right kind of diplomacy and incentives are utilized to diffuse this serious situation. So far, western countries have failed to come up with any solution that could compel Iran to abandon its nuclear plan. Same could be said about North Korea. This country needs food and other necessary things of life desperately. South Korea, United States, Japan, Russia and China-all of these countries- have a stake in keeping North Korea as a non nuclear nation. Though China and Russia are in good terms with the North Korean government yet they have not succeeded in changing the North Korean stand. United States and South Korea might have to deal with North Korean by offering massive economic aid and meet other preconditions as spelled out by North Korea.

Propagating and spreading the American Values: United States has fought many wars against those countries which were deliberately crushing the values held by Americans as sacred and precious-whether it was Germany, Japan or anybody else. Democracy, freedom of speech, freedom of religion and other cardinal principles of American way of life are part and parcel of American dream. Most of the countries in this planet consider America as a role model; a country that they would like to follow in their governing structure. However, there are many countries which do not want to be influenced at all by the American values. Notable among those, are countries which are less developed, highly conservative, poor and not exposed to modern world; many of these countries are Muslim. In this context it must be mentioned that differences in political, social, cultural and religious thoughts are bound to be present and there is nothing wrong about it. What is not admissible is wrong perceptions, ignorant and fanatic religious preaching, oppressive dictatorship and regressive way of life. American ideals may not be easy to follow in this complex structured world, but they are great, worthy to be proud of.

Reflecting on this theme, it must be pointed out that it is in the interest of United States that it should not impose its values on others; it is for others to choose and pick. Differences should be analyzed and appreciated.

A PANORAMIC VIEW OF OUR WORLD

At the conclusion of our study when we look into next two decades of our planet Earth, we feel that only some dramatic upheavals would change the fabric of its texture; in other words, it would not change much compared to its present structure. The dominant change that would be surfacing gradually would be the presence of multiple centers of gravity, areas of influence. Many global powers would be playing the game; there will not be any Super Powers per se.

The whole world would be divided into number of distinct groups or associations. United States, Canada, England, Australia, Japan, South Korea and Philippines would form one group. Russia, China and North Korea would become group number two. India, Indonesia, Brazil and Thailand would form another group. Similarly Arab and other Muslim countries would have their distinct areas of influence. Germany, Japan, China, Brazil and India would become the center of economic growth. Supremacy of economic growth would not be the domain of any single nation; it would be widely distributed among many countries. They would be classified as centers of excellence in their respective fields. The world as such would be moving towards more prosperity and harmony rather than poverty and acrimony.

As we see the future developments in our planet, we can project some of the probable trends for some important countries. We do not see any major changes in Scandinavian countries like Norway, Sweden, Finland and Denmark; they will continue to have higher standards of living but would not be touching bases of military power or global influence. These countries should be considered as very desirable safety cushion for world peace. England, France, Germany and Switzerland would dominate the western front; Italy, Poland, Hungary and Turkey would move towards greater economical strength. The exceptional case among all the countries of the world would be China. The present as well as future Chinese leadership would be focused upon taking the United States position, militarily and economically. Right now there is a long gap between these two countries in those two areas. If there are no disruptions in the Chinese progression, China may very well come at par with the United States in not a distant future. There is no other country which has such a long rounded vision and domineering plans of actions as China has, at this point in world history. It seems like that in military terms, it may equalize with Russia but to exceed United States in all areas of national wealth would not be an easy task.

United States as a leading global power in the world has to adjust its foreign policy for Europe, Asia, South America and Muslim countries in the near future because things would be changing, for sure. It would not be able to play the role of a Super Power; dispersion and diffusion of power would be wide spread among different countries of Europe, Asia and South America. A major role that United States could play effectively in Asia is that of a Peace Maker and provider of all round assistance; it would be appreciated and welcomed by all. Presence of United States is not only necessary but it is essential.

INDEX

The twenty first century will be transformed by the events which are taking shape in the Asian continent. The Asian Age has finally arrived. Political pundits have shifted their attention to the rising sun of Asia. Resurgent countries like China, India and South Korea are taking over the lime light of the western countries. These countries would play the domineering role in global political stage.

We have grouped different countries of Asia into four distinct categories-Allies, Adversaries, Non –Aligned and Unstable. Relations between United States and different Asian countries have been highlighted and some future projections are made. The book describes the pitfalls and clear cut areas where the foreign policy of the United States could operate with confidence and solid returns. A thorough analysis of the existing U.S Foreign Policy across Asian countries has been laid out with clarity and achievable goals

.

AUTHOR'S BIOGRAPHY

Ramesh Raizada is the President of R&R Business Associates-a Consulting firm. He has traveled extensively to different countries of Asia and Europe to collect first hand information on relevant regional and global events. Ramesh major interest covers International Relations and Strategic National Planning. His first book *21st Century World Powers and Changing Alignments (Pub:Jan'12)* provides a detailed description of changed political realities in Asia and what role United States should play under those conditions. His second book: *United States Foreign Policy Across Asia takes the reader to different countries of Asia and points out What is working and what is not and what should be done* by the United States.